The
RUGER .22
AUTOMATIC PISTOL

The
RUGER .22
AUTOMATIC PISTOL

Standard/Mark I/Mark II
Series

DUNCAN LONG

PALADIN PRESS
BOULDER, COLORADO

Also by Duncan Long:

AK47: The Complete Kalashnikov Family of Assault Rifles
AR-15/M16 Super Systems
The AR-15/M16: A Practical Guide
Assault Pistols, Rifles, and Submachine Guns
Build Your Own AR-15
Combat Revolvers
The Complete AR-15/M16 Sourcebook
FN-FAL Rifle
Hand Cannons
Heckler & Koch's Handguns
HK Assault Rifle Systems
Homemade Ammo
The Mini-14: The Plinker, Hunter, Assault, and Everything Else Rifle
Mini-14 Super Systems
Modern Combat Ammunition
Modern Sniper Rifles
Poor Man's Fort Knox
SKS Type Carbines
Streetsweepers: The Complete Book of Combat Shotguns
The Sturm, Ruger 10/22 Rifle and .44 Magnum Carbine
Super Shotguns
The Terrifying Three: Uzi, Ingram, and Intratec Weapons Families

The Ruger .22 Automatic Pistol: Standard/Mark I/Mark II Series
by Duncan Long

Copyright © 1988 by Duncan Long

ISBN 0-87364-488-3
Printed in the United States of America

Published by Paladin Press, a division of
Paladin Enterprises, Inc.
Gunbarrel Tech Center
7077 Winchester Circle
Boulder, Colorado 80301 USA
+1.303.443.7250

Direct inquiries and/or orders to the above address.

Visit our Web site at www.paladin-press.com

Contents

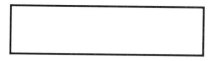

Warning

The technical data presented here, particularly concerning ammunition and the use, adjustment, and alteration of firearms, inevitably reflects the author's beliefs and experience with particular firearms, equipment, and components under specific circumstances which the reader cannot duplicate exactly. The information in this book should therefore be used for guidance only. Neither the author nor the publisher assumes any responsibility for the use or misuse of information contained in this book.

Acknowledgments

A special thanks must go to Linda M. DeProfio for her help in securing information, background history, and photos of Ruger's .22 pistols. Thanks must also go to Sturm, Ruger & Company, Inc., which so graciously gave me firearms to test out during the writing of this book as well as others. Thanks, too, to the many other companies that sent sample products to inspect and test, as well as J. Allan Jones of Omark/CCI, Mike Bussard at Federal Cartridge Company, and John R. Falk at Olin/Winchester, who helped keep me in ammunition while test-firing many of the guns covered in this book.

Special thanks must be given to Peder Lund and his team of skilled editors, proofreaders, and craftsmen at Paladin Press; they all certainly earn their money turning the author's confusing, jumbled manuscripts and dog-eared photos into attractive books.

Finally, thanks to Maggie, Kristen, and Nicholas for helping me finish one more manuscript.

William Batterman Ruger.

Chapter 1

Ruger and His .22 Automatic Pistol

Sturm, Ruger & Company's .22 pistol has become one of the most popular .22 automatics ever made.

There is a number of good reasons for this.

One important reason is that Ruger pistols seldom need to be modified to suit the buyer's needs. This speaks highly of the pistol's good design and the company's ability to manufacture a number of pistol versions, which include varying barrel lengths, sights, and weights, and the introduction of stainless steel models. These "standard" choices allow the purchaser to obtain an out-of-the-box product suitable for varying needs, whether it be for a camp gun, compact "survival" firearm, training gun, target pistol, or even—on occasion—a clandestine weapon for special forces or "spooks." Models of the pistols are available for such use without the help of a gunsmith or the need to spend more money for accessories. This just isn't often the case with most other semiauto pistols.

Another important factor that makes Ruger pistols so popular is reliability. Pistols are often introduced to the public with a few bugs and sometimes continue to function poorly until the owner either has to resort to a gunsmith for "tuning" or discovers which type of ammunition makes it function best.

The Ruger pistol has become one of the most popular .22 automatics ever made because of its high quality and low price tag. Shown here is a late production model of the Standard. (Photo courtesy of Sturm, Ruger and Company.)

Sturm, Ruger & Company didn't market such a pistol. From the first, the company sold a pistol that functioned perfectly right out of the box.

Ruger pistols seldom visit a gunsmith's shop for repair, either. The lack of need for repair again shows how well the pistol is designed and built for a long life of use. And should parts on one of these pistols break through neglect or abuse, they are easily replaced or repaired thanks to a design which makes the Ruger pistols simple to disassemble by a gunsmith—or even the firearm owner himself.

The frosting on the cake is the fact that the pistol has always carried a very low price tag as compared to other .22 pistols capable of giving similar—or even inferior—performance. When introduced in 1949, the pistol sold for $37.50, with the Mark I target pistol carrying a $57.50 price tag when it was introduced a year later. Although pistol prices have climbed during the inflation decades of the seventies and eighties, the pistols have always cost less than such similar .22 pistols as the High Standard and Colt

Although Ruger's new pistol bore a passing resemblance to the old 9mm Luger shown here with its military holster, the .22 pistol was in fact quite different in operation and was designed with modern industrial techniques in mind.

Woodsman. As a result, sales of the Ruger pistols climb while the models marketed by the competition have gradually been discontinued.

Many who first saw the name "Ruger" on the .22 pistol assumed that it was some attempt to mimic the "Luger" trademark used for the German pistols sold in the United States or perhaps a misprint, with an "R" substituted for an "L"; the fact that the Ruger pistol had a somewhat similar appearance to the German pistol (and had the same type of fine balance and point of aim) undoubtedly bolstered this theory.

In fact, the designer, William Batterman Ruger, was born with his name, and any similarity between the two pistols (or other pistols, such as the Lahti P-40 and Nambu) was created by Ruger's use of good design features rather than outright copying for copy's sake. (As subsequent fire-arms have been released by Sturm, Ruger & Company, Ruger has shown that he has a rare combination of firearms genius coupled with artistic talent; this combination has led to the creation of firearms that mimic former models in form while taking advantage of modern manufacturing tech-niques. Ruger's guns look good and are comparatively in-expensive and rugged.)

But Ruger's story isn't one of overnight success; rather, it is one of hard work.

The inventor was born in 1916 and raised in Brooklyn, New York; Ruger was of the fourth generation of German immigrants to be born in America. Unlike the boy's uncles (who had run a shipping firm with routes from New York to Yokohama made by clipper ships), Ruger's father was a lawyer.

Father and son often traveled together on short hunting trips (usually staying in a hunting lodge on the then-remote "wilderness" of Long Island). The boy also spent many summers at his grandfather's home, where he enjoyed shooting a pump-action Remington .22 rifle, a present for his twelfth birthday. (Ruger's grandfather was a portrait art-ist, and it's often speculated that perhaps this is where he got some of his flair for the eye-pleasing line and form of the Ruger firearms.)

Ruger also enjoyed shooting in Brooklyn, despite the fact that shooting was not something easily engaged in within the city. Apparently, Ruger and a close friend, Bill Lett, often fired their rifles in an impromptu shooting gal-lery the two had created—in Lett's basement!

Both of the young men were interested in firearms, and Lett managed to talk his parents into allowing him to pur-chase a government-surplus, .30-40 Krag rifle. Despite the fact that Lett wanted to test-fire the gun in the basement, Ruger (who had seen a .30-'06 in action once and suspected the Krag would have a terrific muzzle blast that would be readily heard by neighbors) convinced him to take the rifle out into the "country"—the open fields beyond the subway line.

Although it is hard to imagine in this day and age, high schools of the 1920s had shooting teams where young men could hone the skills that might be crucial for survival during wartime. Ruger took advantage of this by joining the high-school rifle team and was soon displaying his skills in competition. During this period, Ruger also sifted through all the books he could find in the New York City library and worked up several firearms designs of his own as well.

As Ruger grew older, he gradually added to his small firearms collection, which included several antique Colt black-powder revolvers, a Sharps Creedmore rifle, an '03 Springfield rifle, and a Luger pistol that he often took along while on summer vacations. (As we'll see later, most of these firearms seem to have influenced his firearms design work, especially in regard to the classic lines.)

While in high school, Ruger also had a chance to visit a machine shop from time to time. Seeing metal lathes, drills, and planers in action made a lasting impression on the young man and enlightened him as to how modern machines, from cars to guns, were actually produced.

From high school, Ruger went to prep school in Salisbury, Connecticut. Although student ownership of firearms was banned at the school, Ruger managed to keep one of his prized rifles hidden in an abandoned shack near the campus and often sneaked into the woods for shooting sessions.

School holidays found Ruger haunting machine shops in Brooklyn. He managed to persuade one proprietor of such a business to allow him to actually use some of the motorized tools to create a firearm.

Ruger's design was built around an old Krag rifle, which he modified so that the barrel cycled forward after being fired to reload the firearm. Using an old piece of steel for a backstop, the highly modified rifle was test-fired—and worked! Thinking he had a brand-new invention, the young man applied for a patent for his new design. To Ruger's disappointment, a patent search revealed that the basic idea had been registered nearly a decade before.

After graduating from prep school, Ruger enrolled in the University of North Carolina (at Chapel Hill). It was here that Ruger, working in a basement shop, converted a Savage 99 lever-action rifle into a semiauto firearm (he later wrote a short article about his conversion in *American Rifleman* magazine).

In 1939, after going to college for two years and pursuing a liberal arts degree, Ruger dropped out of college and took a short trip to Europe with his bride, using $10,000 he had just inherited. Following the trip, Ruger settled down in Hartford, Connecticut, and started looking for work, living on what was left of his inheritance.

With his love for, and talent working with, firearms, Ruger tried to get a job with a number of firearms manufacturers, including Savage and Colt. None of the companies would hire him, however, so he ended up working in a small machine shop in Greensboro, North Carolina, making knitting equipment and earning twenty dollars a week.

Ruger spent only a short time working as a machinist. He had applied for work with the military, and the U.S. Army was impressed with his work in converting the Savage rifle to gas operation. Consequently, the military offered him a job as a gun designer at the Springfield Armory in Geneseo, Illinois.

Even though it would seem that this position would have been just the job to suit a man interested in designing firearms, Ruger found the restraints of army bureaucracy not to his liking; things didn't go smoothly, and he quickly became disillusioned in a position where advancement was nearly nonexistent. After working there less than a year, Ruger quit his job at the Springfield Armory.

Ruger again found himself in North Carolina.

Ever an inventor, he soon was at work making parts for a light machine gun of his own design. Once he had finished a working model of his firearm, Ruger took it on the road to show to several manufacturers. Late in 1940, the Auto Ordnance Corporation (which made the Thompson submachine gun) showed interest in a new design that Ruger had made to conform to a memorandum released by the War Department asking for a new military machine gun. In a short time, Ruger found himself working for the company.

By early 1941, Auto Ordnance had set up a machine shop in its Bridgeport, Connecticut, factory for Ruger to work in—for $100 a week—to develop a demonstration prototype of a new .30-caliber machine gun to replace the Browning machine gun. And the new gun was to be produced in just several months' time!

Despite Ruger's hard work to get the gun produced in such a short time, his work with the U.S. military was again to lead to frustration, since the government was continuously changing requirements for its new machine gun. So, although Ruger's machine-gun prototype was actually tested at the Aberdeen Proving Ground in Maryland, it was never accepted. Nevertheless, because of favorable comments made by military testers, Auto Ordnance continued to work on the machine gun for several more years, thinking it might still have a market with the U.S. military.

Despite the fact that the bugs were generally worked out of Ruger's machine gun during this time, World War II was finally winding down (along with the market for innovative new small arms), and the U.S. military was losing interest in adopting a new machine gun. Auto Ordnance decided to table development of the new machine gun, and Ruger was transferred to manufacturing electronic components for the company.

It should be noted that Ruger's time at Auto Ordnance hadn't been wasted. The inventor learned many valuable techniques and lessons that he later used in designing his own firearms. One of the most notable, perhaps, was the way that gun designs created by one of the designers, Douglas Hammond, made use of sheet metal. Hammond's designs used sheet-metal pressings to create halves of parts which were then joined by a weld to create a receiver and grip. This same technique was to be used by Ruger to create the frame of his .22 auto pistol.

Ruger finally quit Auto Ordnance in 1946 and opened up a small manufacturing business of his own. His thinking at the time was that the economy would be on an upswing following World War II, fueling a new construction and manufacturing boom. With this in mind, the Ruger Corporation was created to manufacture quality carpenter's tools to sell to craftsmen.

The young inventor opened his new business in a rented building in Southport, Connecticut. But success was not to come. Though the tools he produced were of high quality, the boom times didn't materialize and what demand there was for tools wasn't for high-quality ones. Sales were poor. Two years later, the company closed. (The tools produced by Ruger during this period have become collector's items. Perhaps of special interest is a hand drill which forms the pattern for the grip of the Ruger .22 automatic pistol.)

Undoubtedly lesser men would have given up and taken a job with an established company. Instead, Ruger was learning from his business setbacks, gaining unique experiences that combined both a newfound business savvy and an intimate knowledge of modern manufacturing techniques and firearms design.

It's probable that Ruger would have persevered in starting a new company on his own to manufacture and market the .22 pistol design he'd developed over several years at Southport. But, at this point, he was to experience a bit of good fortune in his friendship with a neighbor named Alexander M. Sturm.

Sturm was a painter and writer with a colorful history of his own which included working with the OSS (the forerunner to today's CIA) during World War II. Additionally, Sturm had married the granddaughter of President "Teddy" Roosevelt.

Most important to the Sturm/Ruger friendship, Sturm

collected guns for a hobby. This interest in firearms naturally made him rather excited to discover that his neighbor had designed a new pistol. Soon the two men were talking about starting a business to manufacture the guns. Using $50,000 (most of which was Sturm's), the company was soon launched—despite the fact that several businessmen advised the two that a company couldn't be set up on such a small sum of money.

Ruger used his experience in machinery work, as well as his knowledge of metallurgy gained with Auto Ordnance, to create tools to produce the new pistol. Ruger also handled the paperwork, made preliminary sketches and production drawings of the new firearm, and handled various administrative tasks beginning in January 1949. Sturm, who had graduated from Yale Art School, spent much of his time creating ads for the new pistols as well as tending to many of the office chores; additionally, he created the new emblem for the pistol. All the work was carried out in a red barn that had been modernized for use as a machine shop. (This "Old Red Barn" in Southport was purchased in late 1975 by Sturm, Ruger & Company and has since been refurbished and converted into an office by the company's Hawkeye Communications Division.)

The pistol that started the small company wasn't an invention created over a short period of time, though the inventor did apparently gain the insight for the final solution to one tricky part of the firearm's mechanism almost overnight. According to Ruger, he was trying to come up with the final plans for the gun one day when, "almost as a vision, the design details and features came in loud and clear, and I was delighted. I saw the answers and they accomplished everything I wanted. I made my notes completely and correctly. There were two versions of the pistol. I could now take my choice."

Ruger selected the best solution to his design problem and started to build a prototype pistol, filing a patent application in 1946. Ruger continued to work on the prototype until it was finished and "debugged" in 1947.

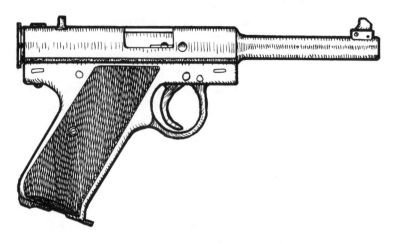

Ruger's prototype .22 pistol differed from the production pistol in a few ways, but it still has the "Ruger look." Most of the basic design features of the final design are present on the test model.

The prototype was a bit different from the final production gun. The prototype had a short, flat-bottomed grip (possibly due to the Colt Woodsman magazine that the inventor had used for his experimental gun); the grip was held in place by one screw rather than the two used on each of the final design grips. The barrel also lacked the taper of the later pistol—a plus—probably because it was an adapted Colt Woodsman barrel. The rest of the pistol, which was made from scratch by Ruger, had more or less the same general lines of the final production gun except that the rear of the bolt had a circular grasping area rather than the two "ears" of the final design. Unlike the final gun, the prototype's receiver was held to the grip frame by two screws.

The production prototype that Ruger built to obtain the final dimensions for his pistols is also of interest. Although the gun is nearly identical to the first pistols sold by Sturm and Ruger, the grips are made of thick, uncheckered wood and held in place by what appear to be two rivets attached to the frame. The rear takedown latch is a rectangular slide release rather than the lever found on the final models. The pistol grip itself had changed considerably from the first experimental gun in which the lower lines had the shape of the hand drill Ruger had designed for his tool company. In addition to making the pistol easier to hold, it increased the magazine capacity and also gave the pistol a nicer balance and eye-pleasing form.

When the fledgling company finally started up in 1949, Ruger assembled and created the machine tools and fixtures needed to build the new gun. His staff included two machinists and ten other men to help turn out parts for the new firearm. Runs of one thousand parts were made at a time so that the company had enough stock on hand to build one thousand pistols when the initial work was done.

When all the parts had been made, the quality of Ruger's work proved to be very high: the pistols could be assembled with little or no hand-fitting (something that was almost unheard of in the firearms industry in 1949). At that point, the firearm was offered for sale to the general public through the mail (which was perfectly legal at the time).

Sturm, Ruger & Company's first ad appeared in *American Rifleman* and the new pistol was blessed with a *very* favorable review by noted gun expert Major General Julian Hatcher in the magazine's "Dope Bag" column. Orders came pouring in for the low-priced, high-quality pistol, which had almost no competition in the marketplace.

The timing of the ad was perfect. Ruger wrote the paychecks for his workers with the last of the $50,000 start-up money on the same day that one hundred assembled pistols were shipped out and the money for them was being deposited in the business's account. Had the review been missing from the magazine or if the ad had appeared a month later, it seems likely that the business might have floundered. Instead, the pistols continued to sell well, with 1,100 guns sold and shipped by the end of 1949.

The gun's ruggedness became well known among users of the firearm, with the guns seldom suffering from parts breakage (at this time, Ruger's "Parts and Service Depart-

The first ad for the .22 Ruger pistol appeared on page 58 of the August 1949 issue of the *American Rifleman*. A good review in the "Dope Bag" section of the magazine augmented the ad's pull.

ment" consisted of a few parts in a cigar box because there were so few calls for replacement parts). As word of mouth spread and favorable reviews continued to be printed in magazines, the company soon found that it was back-ordering guns because the demand was greater than it could keep up with. A notice in the Sturm, Ruger ad in the March 1950 edition of *American Rifleman* read: "Regret—the delay filling orders for the Ruger Automatic Pistol. . . . Because the demand exceeded our expectation, an interval between orders and delivery is temporarily inevitable.

However, we expect to make the Ruger for a long time, and every order will be filled."

The orders were all eventually filled, and the company remained in business. But the great demand for the pistol continued to create a back-order condition until well into the 1970s!

Besides being rugged, another great plus of the new semiauto pistol was that it was low priced. This low price tag was due to the fact that Ruger had designed the gun to take advantage of modern manufacturing techniques, thereby minimizing costly handwork and the milling of steel parts. The pistols sold for only $37.50, while the Colt Woodsman—the principal competition to the new pistol—sold for $60.

The Colt Woodsman had been created by John Browning in 1911; the original pistol was designed for the .22 Short. Colt Firearms purchased the right to make the pistol, and its basic design was reworked by two Colt engineers, F. C. Chadwick and G.H. Tansley, for the .22 LR. The gun was introduced to the public in 1915 as the "Colt .22 Automatic" (it wasn't until 1927 that Colt started calling the pistol the "Woodsman"). Production of the pistol was continued until 1943 when it was discontinued during World War II; production was resumed in 1947.

The Woodsman pistols are good, but their design calls for old production methods which have become prohibitively expensive. Further, the pistol just wasn't as rugged as Ruger's, and the rear sights reciprocated with each shot, making them often shake loose or become hard to zero as play developed in the bolt. Because of this, the Colt Woodsman gradually lost the market to the Ruger pistols, which functioned as well or better than the Colt gun and had a much lower price tag. By 1977, Colt stopped producing its .22 pistol. (Interestingly, in the early 1980s, Iver Johnson introduced a version of the old Woodsman as its Trailsman; the company sold few of the pistols and went bankrupt several years later, which certainly doesn't bode well for those trying to use old methods of producing firearms in the late twentieth century.)

The High Standard pistol was good, but many machining operations were required (including milling out its receiver from the steel stock) so that its price tag was much higher than that of the Ruger. By the mid-1980s, the company went bankrupt.

Much the same thing was to happen to the Ruger pistol's other competition: the High Standard pistol. The High Standard had a number of variations over the years and was known for its accuracy. Unfortunately, these guns also called for a lot of machining, and the rear sights cycled with each shot. The High Standard had a good history. It was used in World War II for training recruits as well as by the OSS, which issued a silenced model for clandestine use; the guns even saw some use in Vietnam. But the U.S. military found that the Ruger pistols were more rugged and reliable, and the public preferred the lower price tag of the Ruger guns. In the mid 1980s, High Standard went bankrupt.

During the first year the Ruger pistol was in production, Jack Boudreau, an employee of Sturm, Ruger & Company, was using the pistol to display his abilities as an excellent and enthusiastic competition shooter. Boudreau started with one of the Standard pistols, modifying its trigger and replacing its rear sight with a "Micro" brand adjustable sight.

In addition to showing off the abilities of the Standard pistol through the high scores Boudreau scored, the customized gun became a sort of test vehicle for a target version of the gun that Ruger had in mind. A year after the introduction of the first model of his first pistol, Ruger took to heart the changes Boudreau had made and created a target pistol with a 6 7/8-inch barrel and an adjustable rear Micro sight. This pistol was introduced as the Mark I in 1950, and the original model of the Ruger pistol became known as the "Standard."

Since the business was going well, Ruger took a much-needed break and left on a hunting trip in the fall of 1951. When the inventor returned to the United States, he found his partner in the hospital, seriously ill. Ten days later, Alex Sturm died at the age of twenty-nine.

To commemorate his friend's death, Ruger's first task was to change the company's heraldic falcon trademark—which had been designed by Sturm—from red to black on the .22 pistol's medallion. This color change has remained in effect with all pistols made since then except for a few commemorative pistols. (It should be noted that the Sturm, Ruger emblem is popularly called the "Ruger Eagle" or "Ruger Hawk" despite the fact that it was apparently designed as a falcon by Sturm. It would seem probable that Ruger himself may call the emblem a "hawk," since his later pistols have such names as Blackhawk and Redhawk.)

There was a precedent for changing a company's emblem to commemorate the passing of a partner; Rolls-Royce had made a similar change several years before Ruger made his change. Given Ruger's love for vintage cars, it would seem likely that the car company inspired his nonetheless thoughtful gesture toward his friend and partner.

Following Sturm's death, the company continued to grow, with Ruger carefully managing it each step of the way. By 1953, Sturm, Ruger & Company had become well established.

With the introduction of the Mark I, a lot of shooters discovered that they were able to shoot very well indeed with the new pistol. One of these shooters was a gunsmith named James Clark, who won the National Civilian .22 Championships (at Camp Perry) a number of times with a Ruger Mark II pistol. Clark was to modify his pistol to suit his needs later, but he won the championship in 1953 with an out-of-the-box Ruger pistol, unmodified except for some black friction tape wrapped around the grips for a better hold!

Despite the facts to the contrary, Sturm, Ruger & Company's competitors spent a lot of time trying to paint the new Ruger pistols as being inferior (thus explaining their lower price tag); in the meantime, the U.S. Army did a little research of its own and discovered that the Ruger pistols were not only rugged, but they had good accuracy. When Sturm, Ruger & Company got the military's new contract for training pistols, it undoubtedly sent a shock wave through the gun manufacturing community.

The period from 1952 to 1953 saw the introduction and suspension in production of a new version of the Ruger Mark I, which had a 5 1/4-inch tapered barrel. For some reason, this model didn't prove to be popular, and it is one of the few Ruger pistols to have been discontinued for reasons other than design improvements. Because this pistol was made for only a short time, it is somewhat of a rarity and often sought by Ruger pistol collectors.

Balancing the discontinuation of the 5 1/4-inch-barreled Mark I in 1953 was the introduction of a new single-action revolver that Ruger had designed. The "Single-Six" revolver looked like a firearm of the old West, and its introduction seemed curious at a time when the industrial trend was toward more modern weapons. In fact, the timing could not have been better, since Hollywood was cranking out Western movies and TV shows and the cowboy/fast-draw craze was sweeping through the shooting public. Adding to Ruger's good fortune was the fact that, even as demand for single-action pistols grew, Colt discontinued its single-action revolvers.

While the new Ruger single-action revolver looked like a copy of an old gun of the West, it was much improved internally. It had a modern, coiled hammer spring rather than the fragile leaf spring of older designs, and most other parts were beefed up as well. Best of all, Ruger had taken advantage of modern production methods so that the guns carried lower price tags. And, like the Standard and Mark I pistols, the new revolver was chambered for the .22 LR, thereby making it inexpensive to shoot.

Sales of the Ruger revolver continued to rocket, with later spin-offs of the gun including one with adjustable sights (in 1964), a model chambered for the .22 WRM (in 1959), and a lightweight model (in 1956). Production of the Single-Six revolver continued from 1953 until 1973—when a new model was introduced. Only the Bearcat revolver, made from 1958 until 1973, proved to be a mediocre seller (and probably not all that bad a seller judging from the amount of time it remained in production).

The year 1953 was also the year in which Ruger took out his first patent on the Standard/Mark I pistols. The patent search and application submitted in 1946 had shown that such a patent wouldn't infringe on previous inventions. Patent number U.S. 2655839 was for Ruger's unique .22 semiauto pistol, which he constructed using modern industrial methods.

Ruger continued to add new products to his company's lineup. Two years after the Single-Six was released, a somewhat heavier single-action revolver, the Blackhawk, was added to the Ruger lineup. Chambered for centerfire cartridges, this gun captured even more of the single-action market, with the heavier guns being capable of taking on such tasks as hunting or even self-defense. Ruger therefore started cutting into two new and growing markets. In 1963, a magnum version of the gun was released to the public as the "Super Blackhawk."

Ruger's guns sold, and sold well. By 1959, Sturm, Ruger & Company had outgrown its original plant. A move was made to a larger building; this was good only for less than a year, at which time a new addition to the plant had to be added, doubling its size in an effort to keep production up with demand.

New firearms designs continued to roll out of the Sturm, Ruger & Company plant, with Ruger overseeing the work of teams of designers. Unlike many other successful men who either decide to stop advancing or, at the other extreme, have trouble delegating authority, Ruger displayed flair both in design work and business. The company stayed vital and growing.

Every few years saw the introduction of completely new weapons, with variations of one or another coming out yearly from Sturm, Ruger & Company. The year 1959 saw the introduction of the .44 Carbine; 1963, the Hawkeye Pistol (a single-action pistol which has since been discontinued); 1964, the Model 10/22 (which has become one of the best-selling .22 rifles ever made); 1967, the Number One single-shot rifle series; 1968, the M-77 bolt-action rifle series; 1971, a series of double-action, law-enforcement-style revolvers; 1972, the Old Army black powder-revolver; 1975, the Mini-14 series of .223 rifles (which was a hit in sporting, military, police, and survival markets); in 1977, the Over and Under double-barreled shotgun in 20-gauge (with a 12-gauge introduced in 1982); 1979, the Redhawk double-action revolver family; 1983, the Model 77/22 bolt-action .22; 1986, the introduction of the new GP-100 series of revolvers; 1987, the Mini-30 (a Mini-14 spin-off chambered for the 7.62x39mm cartridge) and Super Redhawk revolver; and in 1988, the P-85 9mm automatic pistol (along with a new plant in Prescott, Arizona, to manufacture it). Such rapid firearms development and marketing has been unheard of in the firearms history, causing Bill Ruger to become a legend in his own time.

To the chagrin of marketing analysts everywhere, Ruger does not pay anyone to do "marketing studies" of what types of firearms he should develop. Rather he makes what he thinks sounds good! Thus far, Ruger has proven to be a better judge of things than are surveys and computer studies. And, by doing things the way Ruger sees, Sturm, Ruger & Company has been setting trends in the firearms industry rather than following them.

Ruger once told an interviewer that "When manufacturers go around making surveys and asking people what they want, what they're really saying is that they don't understand the business they're in. Our business is more than a business, it is like some sports—it has a heart. I mean, guns aren't just something you make like tools or chairs or some other utility objects. Guns are valued possessions and provoke all sorts of emotional responses in people. If the manufacturer doesn't know what makes a really appealing gun, then he isn't going to have much success. I can't say I know all about it—I wish I could—but I do love guns, and that's been a big help."

During the late 1950s, the Mark I pistol was showing up on target ranges and would become, more or less, a standard fixture on pistol ranges throughout the United States by the mid 1960s. Besides being accurate, the pistols had also gained a reputation for being rugged and dependable (something rival pistols couldn't always claim). Stories of test-firings of 50,000 rounds without failure to feed or any parts breakage make a lasting impression on those who plan to purchase a target pistol.

With such accuracy, dependability, and durability, it is little wonder that the U.S. Army and Air Force were soon purchasing thousands of the pistols for use in training troops; Sturm, Ruger & Company made several thousand of them in 1957 with the standard Mark I 6 7/8-inch tapered barrel (these guns were stamped "U.S."). A few of these pistols were also modified by Army armorers and found their way into the hands of the U.S. Army Marksmanship Unit at Ft. Benning, Georgia, for use by the Army pistol teams. Apparently, the armorers found that a tight chamber 0.0005 of an inch smaller than the SAAMI maximum cartridge dimension and a forcing cone with a 12-degree included angle gave best results. (SAAMI [Sporting Arms and Ammunition Manufacturer's Institute] is the U.S. organization that maintains standard specs for chamber and cartridge case dimensions.)

Adding to the solid reputation the Mark I was getting from its showing on the target range was an article by Carl J. Davis that appeared in the June 1962 issue of *American Rifleman*. His article described procedures for rebarreling the Mark I; a 1-in-14 twist barrel with tight chamber could give one-inch groups at 50 yards with quality ammunition. (Most target pistols of the time were only capable of this type of performance at 25 to 30 yards!)

Care had to be used with such pistols, since too large a cartridge might slam-fire upon chambering. To overcome this problem, Army and other target shooters often used a gauge (often made from the chamber end of a Ruger barrel) to check the size of ammunition before it was used.

Davis followed up his article in the September 1964 issue of *American Rifleman* with another on converting the Ruger to the .22 Short cartridge (which was used for international rapid-fire pistol competition). Davis found that a 1-in-24 twist gave best accuracy with the small cartridges and that the 12-degree forcing cone angle that had proved best with the .22 LR also worked well with the .22 Short. A High Standard magazine was used to feed the shorter round into the modified Ruger pistol. (The .22 Short is not as accurate as the .22 LR, but Davis was still able to achieve one-inch groups at 25 yards with converted pistols.)

A number of pistolsmiths started modifying the Ruger pistols for target shooters. Foremost of these was Jim Clark of Shreveport, Louisiana. Working on a custom basis, his work generally consisted of replacing the barrel with a heavy Douglas barrel with a 1-in-14 twist and a 12-degree forcing cone. Additional work included adding a wide, serrated trigger (with an over-travel stop), smoothing out the action, and installing more precise rear sights. Usually a new follower was placed in standard magazines to hold the bolt open after the last shot had been fired.

Sturm, Ruger & Company was to lose some of its share of the target pistol market when High Standard introduced a pistol with a military grip in the late 1960s. By the early 1980s, much of the lost market was regained after High Standard went out of business and the expensive Smith and Wesson Model 41 target pistol became harder to obtain. At any rate, the guns sold to target shooters were only a very small portion of the sales made by Sturm, Ruger & Company.

By 1963, Sturm, Ruger & Company was finding the demand for its firearms so great that it needed to expand its manufacturing space again. This expansion was carried out by creating a subsidiary company, Pine Tree Castings, which would handle all the investment casting work for Ruger. The new plant, located in Newport, New Hampshire, was completed in 1964. Pine Tree Castings has become the largest producer in the United States of investment castings for firearms, because Sturm, Ruger & Company uses more castings in its firearms than all the rest of the firearms industry combined. By 1984, Pine Tree Castings had grown to twenty-two times its original size, and a second casting division, Uni-Cast, was created in Manchester, New Hampshire, to cast additional gun parts for Ruger and other companies.

Investment castings are one of the reasons that Sturm, Ruger & Company can create low-cost firearms. The process, also known as the "lost wax process," creates parts by forming wax models from relatively inexpensive molds and then placing fine, sandlike material around the wax model. These sand-coated pieces are baked in order to melt out the original wax model, and steel is then poured into the empty sand molds. After the steel has cooled and hardened, the sand mold is removed, leaving a nearly finished piece that needs only a minimum of machining to bring it to final shape and size. (For a look at investment castings being made, as well as an interesting look at Bill Ruger and his company, the reader is directed to the sixty-minute video cassette, *Conversations with Bill Ruger,* available from the Blacksmith Corporation for $60. See Appendix B for more information.)

Investment castings save a lot of expensive machining work since the wax model can be very detailed; even though most other companies still mill parts from solid blocks of steel, Sturm, Ruger & Company simply casts the part and does some finishing work. Besides being faster to make, the parts are also more durable than milled parts since the crystalline structure of the steel tends to be more complete in the investment casting, thereby making it stronger. An additional plus is that steel alloys that aren't readily machined can be readily cast to create tough gun parts that are impossible to make any other way.

A good example of how much stronger an investment casting can be was made by Sturm, Ruger & Company when it tested the bolts of the Springfield 03-A3 rifle, a Mauser, and a Ruger M-77 rifle (which uses an investment-cast bolt). The Springfield and Mauser 98 were found to fail with 15,000 and 18,000 pounds of pressure; the Ruger M-77 bolt, basically identical to the bolts in these two firearms except for being an investment casting, didn't fail until more than 25,000 pounds of pressure were reached.

While the Ruger .22 automatic pistol doesn't have nearly as many investment castings as other Ruger guns, it does have several which help to keep the production costs down when combined with stamped and screw-machined parts, plastic grips, a receiver made of steel tubing, and a frame made of two pressings (welded together, though it's almost impossible to tell where the weld is made due to the care taken in polishing the pistol).

In early 1978, Ruger brought out a stainless steel version of the Mini-14, and in 1982 introduced the Ranch Rifle version with a scope mount molded into its receiver. By the mid 1980s, the demand for all Mini-14 versions had become so great that Sturm, Ruger & Company plants were hard-pressed to keep up with demand for just the rifle. A new plant devoted just to the manufacture of the Mini-14 rifle was opened.

Sturm, Ruger & Company announced that it was ready to produce its millionth Standard automatic pistol during the company's thirtieth anniversary in 1979. At this time, the company displayed a commemorative, one-millionth Standard pistol, which had been hand engraved, at the 1980 SHOT show in San Francisco. The pistol was again displayed with the Ruger Collectors Association in 1980 at the Spring Sahara Antique Arms Show in Las Vegas, Nevada.

The millionth Standard was presented to the ISDF (International Shooter Development Fund) at the Gun Collectors Open Meeting on April 13. The meeting took place during the Annual Meetings of the National Rifle Association in Kansas City, Missouri, where the pistol was on display to the public for the last time.

The ISDF then auctioned off the pistol, which had been beautifully engraved by Ray Viramontez (of Dayton, Ohio) and sported ivory grips made by Ron Lang (of Hays, Kansas). The pistol bore a serial number of "1000000" and had the old red falcon medallion that appeared on the original pistol; the signature of William Ruger was also rolled into the barrel of the pistol. Roll markings were gold inlayed, and the pistol was cased in a velvet-lined, glass-topped walnut box, which bore an engraved silver plate on its lid.

Proceeds from the ISDF auction went to the U.S. Shooting Team, and the winner of the sealed bidding was Austin M. Wortley, Jr., who was the chairman of Penguin Industries (located in Coatesville, Pennsylvania). The winning bid was $27,200.

After nearly thirty-three years of continuous manufacture of the Standard and Mark I variations, the Mark II variation of the Mark I pistol was introduced in 1982. The Mark II variants replaced the original models and were basically refinements of the parent guns, with many of the internal parts actually being interchangeable. The basic improvements of the Mark II are in the addition of a bolt stop which

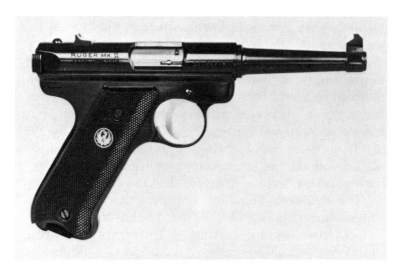

Still one of the Sturm, Ruger and Company's big sellers, the Ruger pistol has been modified slightly to become the Mark II, shown here in the "Standard" version. (Photo courtesy of Sturm, Ruger and Company.)

was activated after the last shot was fired, as well as manually; a new, easier-to-insert magazine with one-round larger capacity (holding a total of ten cartridges); a new trigger shape with an internal pivot retainer; a safety that could be activated when the pistol was being cocked; and a cutout at the rear of the receiver tube to allow easier grasping of the bolt when it was being pulled back to load the gun.

A limited run of five thousand Standard pistols was made in January 1982. These pistols bore Ruger's signature over the top of the receiver along with the caption, "1 of 5000." The pistols were made of stainless steel and bore the red falcon emblem on the grip (which appeared on the first pistols) rather than the current black medallion. Each pistol also had a wooden "salt-cod" style box made for it since such boxes were used to mail the original pistols to customers. There were to be no more Standard or Mark I pistols produced by Sturm, Ruger & Company. All new .22s were to be of the new Mark II configuration.

One of Sturm, Ruger & Company's competitors for the .22 handgun market is Browning Firearms. Like Colt and

High Standard, Browning has found the competition tough, but the company has managed to stay in business thanks to its sales of rifles, shotguns, and 9mm pistols. Browning got into the .22 pistol market in 1962 with the introduction of three .22 pistols that outwardly resembled the Colt Challenger version of the Woodsman (designed years earlier by the company's founder, John Browning).

The new pistols were slightly changed from the Woodsman internally, with the work being done under the direction of Bruce Browning, the grandson of John Browning. One of these three new pistols was the Challenger, which was a target pistol; another was marketed as the "Nomad" (the economy model), while the third was known as the "Medalist" (for competition shooters). The pistols were followed in 1970 by the International Medalist (which was basically a Medalist pistol with thinned fore-end and a thinner grip). All versions of the pistol were discontinued in 1974; the basic reason: they couldn't be produced at a price competitive with the Ruger Mark I.

Browning tried again with the Challenger II, marketed in 1976. The new pistol was a slightly modified version of the original, which had been overhauled by Joe Badali and again bore an outward resemblance to the old Colt Woodsman. To help keep costs down, this pistol was manufactured in the United States rather than in Belgium.

By 1982, Browning was marketing the Challenger III, which used a lightweight alloy frame in order to cut production costs. In the mid 1980s, the Challenger II was modified to become the Challenger III Sporter, with a low-cost version of the pistol with plastic grip panels and a simplified rear sight introduced as the "Buck Mark 22" in 1985. The Silhouette Buckmark and Varmint models introduced in 1987 replaced the Challenger III in another effort to keep prices down.

But, despite the scrambling that Browning has done, the Ruger Target pistols still enjoy a much lower price tag than do Browning's. Thus, the Browning guns gain only a small portion of the market otherwise commanded by the Ruger guns.

In 1984, another company, AMT (Arcadia Machine & Tool), tried to cut into some of the Sturm, Ruger & Company's market by introducing two new stainless steel guns under the Lightning trademark. One was a copy of the Mark I .22 pistol, and the other was a copy of the 10/22 carbine (such copies were legal to make due to the fact that patent rights had run out on the two firearms).

The AMT Lightning pistol is different from the Ruger gun only in several cosmetic changes, an adjustable trigger, and scope-mount cuts to the top of the receiver. The guns look a bit different from the parent design thanks to a spike to the front of the trigger guard, which aids in two-handed holds, and a slab-sided, rather than tubular, receiver.

AMT also marketed a line of receiver/barrel assemblies when the pistol was first introduced. These assemblies were offered for both the AMT gun as well as the Ruger, the idea being that an owner could quickly disassemble his pistol and put a longer or shorter barrel on it to suit different shooting needs. Apparently, most American shooters didn't experience such a need since the units didn't sell well and are no longer offered. (Possibly the fact that the upper receiver of the Ruger design bears the serial number added to the problems in selling these as well, since all the paperwork required to purchase a complete firearm was needed just to buy one of the receiver/barrel units.)

Both the AMT Lightning pistol and rifle versions of the Ruger guns work well; many shooters, however, feel that the guns made by Sturm, Ruger & Company generally outperform the copies. While AMT did have a slight edge in the number of barrel lengths offered, the company has now cut back on those choices, while Ruger has increased its offerings. Adding to AMT's problems is the fact that its guns are burdened with higher price tags than those offered by Ruger. All in all, it is probable that AMT has not cut into Ruger's market to any great extent.

Ruger's .22 automatic pistol will remain popular for

some time, and it would seem probable that it will be around well into the twenty-first century or longer. The pistol's accuracy and reliability, coupled with a number of accessories and the firearm's low price tag, make it first choice for those who are looking for a .22 pistol.

As to other firearms produced by Ruger, there is no end in sight, as there are many firearms "in the works" at Sturm, Ruger & Company. During the next few years, it is probable that the inventor will pull more firearms out of his design team's bag of tricks.

In the meantime, Sturm, Ruger & Company has gone public; the business, however, is still tightly run by William Ruger. His close attention to details continues to steer the course of the company and the quality of the arms it produces. (When officials at Sturm, Ruger & Company are questioned about design changes in various firearms or why a firearm has been discontinued or added to the company's lineup, the answer given is often simply, "Because that's the way Bill wants it.")

Sturm, Ruger & Company celebrates its fortieth anniversary in 1989, with more than ten million guns having flowed from its factories. In fact, six models of firearms have sold more than one million each (the M-77, Old and New models of the single-action revolver, the 10/22, and the double-action Security-, Service-, and Speed-Six revolvers), not to mention the Standard/Mark I pistols.

One of the company's big sellers continues to be the .22 automatic pistol which is nearly identical to that first introduced in 1949. The inventor of the pistol seems to have a fond place in his heart for the gun as well. When asked in a recent interview about which of his firearms was his favorite, Ruger replied, "Well, I'm quite fond of the No. 1 single-shot rifle and the over-under shotgun, but most of all, I get sentimental over that first Standard Model .22 pistol that started things going."

In a 1975 presentation banquet in which William Ruger was chosen for the Handgunner of the Year Award, Lee Jurrus, the award's sponsor, said of Bill Ruger, "To date, his company has been the most successful new gun company of the century."

It appears probable that Sturm, Ruger & Company will soon become the most successful commercial gun manufacturer in history.

Chapter 2

Variations of the Ruger .22 Pistols

There are many variations of the Ruger pistols, but all are basically the same. The grip frame and internal trigger group are nearly identical on all production models, ranging from the first off the assembly line to modern guns.

About the only awkward thing about the well-designed pistol is—for lefties—the placement of its safety. Although William Ruger is left handed, the safety is on the left of the frame, where it is easily reached only by a right-hand hold. While this seems a bit odd in an age of ambidextrous safeties, releases, slide releases, and you-name-it on guns, it really makes little difference on a target/plinker pistol like the Ruger .22. (And many a gun expert—including gun guru Jeff Cooper—has suggested that careful handling of a firearm makes the safety superfluous anyway. Keeping the finger clear of the pistol trigger until the shot is fired prevents accidental discharge even if the safety is in the "fire" position.)

Other than the safety, the gun is more or less "ambidextrous," with the magazine release, bolt ears, and the bolt release readily worked with either a left- or right-hand hold (lefties find that the bolt release is easily engaged with the forefinger—something right-handers never think looks correct).

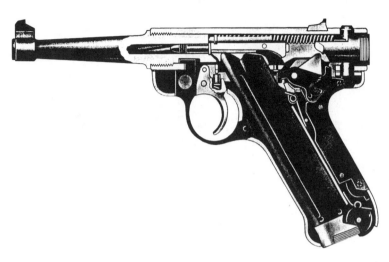

Sectional view of the Ruger Standard pistol. (Drawing courtesy of Sturm, Ruger and Company.)

Because Ruger has made a number of improvements to his pistol since it was first introduced, most things anyone has ever had a gripe about, such as the lack of a bolt hold-open device, has been corrected.

The original Standard and Mark I pistols lacked a bolt hold-open function after the last shot was fired. Although some aftermarket magazines were made with longer-than-normal magazine followers that caught the bolt and held it open after the last shot, this was not satisfactory, since removing the magazine was harder and the bolt clanked shut when the magazine was finally pried loose. The modified magazine did make it possible to tell when the pistol was empty, however, and avoided the annoyance of trying to fire the pistol and being greeted by a click rather than a blast after losing track of how many shots had been fired. A bolt hold-open device was also needed by those who used the pistol in competition shooting, where firing line rules require the pistol be locked open after a round of shooting is over.

The Mark II bolt can be locked open manually at any time by retracting the bolt and pushing the bolt hold-open lever up. The bolt is also automatically locked open after the last shot is fired when the magazine's follower hits an internal engagement. Unlike the magazine modified with a longer follower, the bolt hold-open device keeps the bolt back when the magazine is removed. Once a loaded magazine is inserted, it is easy to quickly reload by pushing down on the bolt release (or retracting the bolt by pulling on its "ears" and releasing it). This causes the bolt to slam forward, stripping off a round from the magazine and leaving the Ruger .22 ready to fire.

In addition to making the pistol quick to reload, the bolt hold-open feature is also ideal for cleaning the pistol when full disassembly is impractical or not really necessary. (The Standard/Mark I pistols enjoy the same ease of quick cleaning since they can be locked open for cleaning with the safety.)

The rear sights vary among the Mark I, and Mark II variants have Micro sights that are adjustable for windage and elevation with small screwdrivers (two different-sized blades being needed); the Standard models have a fixed sight (which can be drifted for windage with a punch).

Front sights show greater variance, with the Standard and Target models generally having a front sight band that holds a blade in place. The Bull Barrel model has a sight base that is screwed into the top of the barrel and then holds the blade in place. Both the Target and Bull Barrel models have blades with sharper back angles; the Standard has a squared base with a less extremely angled blade atop it.

The Standard-style front sight gives a fairly good sight picture and is less apt to catch in most holsters. Even though the sharp rear angle of the Target and Bull Barrel front sights creates a light/shadow contrast that makes the front sight easy to find in almost any type of lighting condition, the sharp point created on the rear end of the front sight can give a lot of wear and tear to holsters or can get hooked in clothing if care isn't taken when using it. (These are generally minor considerations for most owners of the target pistols, however.)

One modification of the front sight occasionally seen with both types of sights is the rounding off of the top rear portion of the sight to make a simple ramp blade like that found on most other sporting firearms. This work is easily done with a file (and a little touch-up blue with blued-steel guns), making it a suitable project for an amateur gunsmith. Some thought should be given before launching into this project, however; such a front sight doesn't produce as sharp a shadow/light contrast when so modified, so that shooting with such a pistol isn't as quick as with a standard front sight.

Sturm, Ruger & Company's quality control is such that the sights are generally pretty well zeroed as they come from the factory; many shooters never have to adjust the sights on Standard models. Target shooters may find that various types of ammunition dictate changes in elevation, and range conditions may require windage adjustments.

Should adjustment be necessary on fixed sights, changing ammunition is one way to very easily change elevation. Should this be impractical, filing down the front sight or the depth of the rear blade can be very carefully done to raise or lower the point of impact. The secret to such work is to remove minimal amounts of metal while testing the changes at a range. Filing down the front sight will raise the point of impact, while lowering the rear sight's notch will lower the point of impact.

If a Standard pistol consistently hits to the left or right of a target regardless of crosswinds or other conditions, the pistol's rear sight can be drifted to one side to compensate. The work should be done with a punch that has a brass or plastic end so that it doesn't mar the pistol's finish. Drifting the rear sight to the right or left will move the point of impact in the *opposite* direction. This adjustment should only be made once to zero the pistol or when a drop or blow has moved the rear sight out of alignment. In crosswinds, windage should be made by aiming upwind to the target since moving the sight will gradually loosen it so that it won't hold zero. (Should a shooter discover the sight won't stay in place on an old, abused Standard, the sight can be "staked" in place by a gunsmith, or a drop of lacquer or nail polish can be used to lock it in place.)

One big plus of the Ruger pistol's sights is that they remain stationary as its inner bolt recoils. Coupled with the .22's light recoil, it is possible to keep the pistol on target for rapid second or third shots without having the rear sight become a blur of motion. Such capability is similar to that of semiauto rifles and has undoubtedly given hunters something for the pot rather than a missed opportunity on more than one occasion.

This design also keeps the rear sights from going out of alignment as is often the case with other pistols having the sights on a reciprocating slide; even the low recoil of a .22 can cause a lot of strain to a precision sight during the cycling of a semiauto's action. Owners of Colts and High Standards also often discover that their shots will wander, either as the slide becomes loose with wear or on new guns that have left the manufacturer with a bit of built-in play.

Good sights may not be of help to older shooters or those who are a bit farsighted. They may discover that their arm just isn't long enough to use the sights of any pistol with any great ease. In such a case, mounting a scope on the Ruger auto pistol makes sense.

Those using the pistol for hunting may also find that using a scope has some merit; the innate accuracy of most Ruger .22s certainly justifies such a mounting. Many have found that a scoped Ruger pistol can do anything a .22 rifle can, but it is considerably lighter to carry in the field. About the only drawback is that some ammunition may give slightly lower performance with the pistol's shorter barrel. (This isn't always the case, however, especially with the longer barrels available for the pistol. Many types of .22 ammunition will achieve peak velocities with a 10-inch barrel. Thus, a Ruger with a 6- to 10-inch barrel may actually send bullets out with as great a velocity as a rifle with a 16-, 18-, or 20-inch barrel.)

The top of the AMT Lightning receiver is grooved for

easy scope mounting but this isn't the case with current production models of the Sturm, Ruger pistols. Fortunately, there are many good scope mounts readily available to Ruger owners (more on these in a later chapter).

The Ruger pistol operates in a simple blow-back manner, with the recoil produced by the .22 cartridge propelling the spring-loaded bolt backward shortly after the bullet has left the barrel. This action cocks the hammer, and the extractor pull holds the empty cartridge in place as the bolt recoils. The empty brass is pushed out the ejection port of the pistol when it hits the ejector on the side of the receiver. When the bolt's rearward movement is stopped by the recoil spring and bolt-stop pin, the spring pushes the bolt forward and a round is stripped from the magazine and pushed into the chamber; the extractor slips over the rim of the shell. Another pull on the trigger will release the hammer, which collides with the rear of the firing pin; the firing pin, in turn, strikes the rear of the cartridge rim to fire it. When the magazine is empty, the Standard and Mark I bolts simply close on an empty chamber; with the Mark II series of guns, the magazine follower activates the bolt hold-open mechanism, which locks the bolt back. Operation of the pistol is simple but efficient. It should be noted that bullets leaving the gun have as much velocity as those from single-shot guns with comparable barrel lengths and slightly greater velocity than revolvers since gas is leaked from the gap between the chambers and forcing cone of wheel guns.

One interesting innovation with the Ruger pistols is the placement of the hammer in a low position where extra force is needed to push it back during recoil. This, in effect, makes the hammer function to reduce the rate of recoil which gives a bit more time for rounds to feed up to the lip of the magazine before the bolt strips them off for chambering. This helps prevent the jams that plague some similar pistols.

Although the pistol grip/frame of the Ruger pistol is made of steel, it is quite different from the cast and/or milled frames of nearly all other handguns. On the Ruger pistol, the frame is made of two heavy sheet steel pressings that are welded together along their edges and then carefully ground and burnished. In addition to minimizing the time and expense taken to create the frame, this construction also makes the frame lightweight. (Although this light weight causes absolutely no problems in the field, care should be taken when working on the pistol in a vise. Many amateur gunsmiths have discovered the hard way that over-tightening a vise on the pistol can warp or even collapse the frame.)

It is also interesting that most guns made with stamping look cheap with spot welds giving them a cut-rate military look; by way of contrast, the Ruger stamped frame has a classic elegance all its own, and the welds are apparent only upon close inspection of the inside of the frame.

The Ruger pistol's box magazine is like that of most other pistols in that it uses a standard coiled spring to push the magazine follower and the rounds above it toward the lips of the magazine. One good design feature of the Ruger magazine is that it's slanted at such an angle as to make the rims of the .22 cartridges overlap and support each other so that they don't "nose down" in the magazine. This results in reliable feeding as well as a very comfortable grip angle.

Occasionally, some Ruger pistol owners complain that its magazines are hard to load. Often this comes about because the shooter tries to load magazines by pulling the follower button on the side of the magazine all the way down, holding it in place as shells are put in one at a time. A better bet is to pull down just a bit on the follower button, place a shell in the magazine, and then release the button while another shell is picked up. The button is then pulled down just enough to insert another cartridge, and the cycle is repeated until ten cartridges are in the gun. At that point, if the shooter wants to carry the maximum number of cartridges and will be shooting right away, another shell can be put into the chamber and the full magazine inserted, giving eleven bangs before the gun is empty.

(If, however, the gun isn't to be fired right away, it is generally a safer practice to keep the chamber of the pistol empty and hand-cycle a round off the magazine when getting ready to shoot. The only time this isn't a wise practice is when you're in "snake country" or using the pistol for self-defense.)

In addition to standard blued-steel versions of the .22 pistol, Ruger also markets stainless steel models. Sturm, Ruger & Company currently denotes stainless steel versions of its guns by placing a "K" prefix on the gun's number; this makes it possible to readily see whether any given model is stainless or blued steel.

PISTOL VERSIONS

When these stainless steel versions are taken into consideration, there is a huge number of variants—enough to make a collector's mouth drool. There is a Ruger pistol to suit almost any need. The more common versions of the Sturm, Ruger & Company pistols are as follows.

The "Standard" Pistol

The "Standard" designation wasn't actually used by Sturm, Ruger & Company until the introduction of the Mark I series, which created a need for naming the original pistols. The Standard was the first marketed by Sturm, Ruger in 1949 and was produced until 1982. Very early pistols had a red falcon on the left grip panel; those made after late 1951 have a black emblem, which was adopted after the death of Sturm. Guns made between 1951 and 1971 have the emblem on the left grip; post-1971 Rugers have the emblem on the right.

The change in medallion placement from the left grip to the right came about when the original forming dies for the two pistol-frame halves wore out in 1971. At that time, the small cutout at the bottom of the pistol grip was moved to the left of the pistol and the follower button changed to that side; the medallion was moved to the right (making identification of the change easy). The new frame style was desig-

The Standard with a 4¾-inch barrel was the original pistol marketed by Sturm, Ruger in 1949. The first pistols had a red falcon on the left grip panel; those made after late 1951 have a black emblem. (Photo courtesy of Sturm, Ruger and Company.)

Early Standards had their falcon emblem on the left grip, with the right (shown here) plain. The falcon was moved to the right grip in 1971. (Photo courtesy of Sturm, Ruger and Company.)

nated the "A-100," or "New Model." Grips of the New Model and Old Model Rugers are not interchangeable, and the Old Model magazines won't fit in the New Model. However, New Model magazines can have the magazine button switched from the left side to the right by disassembling the magazine and reversing the follower.

(When added to a part number, the "0" designation generally denotes a change in specifications. The two 0s in the A-100 designation would seem to denote two changes, but it is probable that this denotes one change for each pistol half. This is further born out by the A-10000 designation of the next change in the pistol frame for the Mark II series.)

Apparently, the reason for changing the follower button from one side to the other was to accommodate a bolt hold-open device, which Ruger seems to have had in mind for some time. The hold-open design change required that the follower button be on the left so the switch apparently was made to lay the groundwork for the final modification. In effect, Ruger was "planning ahead" by more than a decade for the final change in the pistol's design.

A late-production model of the Standard with a 6-inch barrel is shown here. The silver falcon on a black background appeared on the pistol grip. (Photo courtesy of Sturm, Ruger and Company.)

Strangely enough, the red falcon emblem was originally changed to a black bird on a silver background; at some point during production and without any fanfare, the emblem was reversed to a silver bird on a black background. The exact reason for this is unknown, but the change suggests that the method of producing the grips may have changed at this point or that a changeover to a new grip material occurred.

Standard grips (as well as those of the Mark I) are made with sharp diamond checkering molded into them. A hard, rubberlike material, Butaprene, is used in their manufacture. Sturm, Ruger & Company also offered optional walnut grips for both the Standard and the Mark I; at first, these were mounted on pistols by the factory. Later, customers had to order the walnut grips as replacement parts since the company couldn't keep up with the extra work caused by setting up "custom" pistols on the assembly line.

Both the Standard and Mark I were sold with 9-round magazines. The base plate of the magazine, as well as the trigger of both guns, was made of a zinc-alloy metal with the trade name Zamak; both had a silver-colored finish that contrasted nicely with the blued finish of the guns.

Very early guns have a nonbeveled ejection port; those made after the introduction of the Mark I generally have beveling. Early models of the Standard also had narrower rear sight dovetails milled into the receiver than subsequent pistols. Between serial numbers 2,500 and 2,800, the bolt and firing pin were altered slightly to simplify production and make the pin considerably more durable. Somewhere around serial number 2,500 (possibly at the time the bolt and firing pin were changed), the loose recoil spring guide, spring, and retainer parts were being produced as an assembly with a split at the end of the guide acting as a rivet to hold the parts together. It would seem probable that other minor changes in part structure and dimensions were made throughout the production of these pistols in order to improve functioning and simplify production.

Two models of the Standard were made: the original

Ruger pistol (which was later designated the RST4—Ruger STandard 4 3/4-inch barrel—in company literature) and the RST6 version of the Standard (with a 6-inch barrel), which was introduced in the autumn of 1954. Twists for the barrels were 1 turn per 16 inches for early models, with the more accurate 1-in-14, 6-groove rifling being adopted in later pistols.

Triggers on the Standard pistols have improved since the early ones, which generally have a lot of slack and over-travel and occasionally a bit of creep. When the Mark I pistols were introduced, the new Mark I triggers were made available as options for the Standard pistols so both RST4s and RST6s may be found with this trigger. This, coupled with a number of aftermarket triggers that were available during the period the guns were made, means that many Standard pistols with very good pulls will be encountered. (Since the rear Micro sight of the Mark I was offered as an option for the Standard pistols, many of the RST4s and RST6s are light-barreled Mark Is for all intents and purposes.)

Serial numbers of the Standard models started with "1" (all the number 1s remain in William Ruger's collection) and were numbered consecutively as they were made until the Mark I variants were produced. At that point, the two guns shared the same series of numbers so that there are gaps in numbering in each of the variants.

The last Standard pistol was made December 31, 1981.

The Mark I

Introduced in December 1950 with actual deliveries made early in 1951 (causing a bit of confusion to those trying to place a date as to when the gun was first made), the Mark I series was manufactured until 1982 and had a catalog listing of T678. The Mark I is basically the Standard pistol with the addition of a heavier, 6 7/8-inch tapered barrel (with a 1-in-14 twist), a modified trigger with stops to lower over-travel and slack, and target sights (the rear sight being click-adjustable and the front having a greater undercut for more light contrast). In addition to being sold to civilians, thousands of these pistols were sold to the U.S. Army and Air Force for training purposes; these guns have special "U.S." markings on the receiver to distinguish them from the regular pistols.

Early versions of the pistol had the red falcon emblem on the left grip plate; those made after late 1951 have the black emblem on the left grip plate. In 1971, the emblem was transferred to the right grip panels when the New Model A-100 frames were first made. Production pistols were sold with the hard rubber black grips identical to those of the Standard model. Walnut grips (with or without thumb rests incorporated into their design) were originally offered as an option; but, in order to keep up with demand, such options were discontinued and the grips offered as parts that customers could purchase and use to replace the stock grips.

A muzzle brake that was quite effective in reducing muzzle climb was introduced by Ruger in 1955 and made available as an aftermarket accessory. The brake was simply a metal tube with a large, bullet-shaped cutout in its top (flat end toward the rear), which diverted gases upward upon firing the pistol. It was secured to the pistol by replacing the front sight pin with a slightly longer one that extended into the top of the brake. Unfortunately, the useful device has since been discontinued by the company.

Serial numbers of the Mark I fall within the Standard series so that gaps in numbering are taken up by the Standard serial numbers. Because of potential product liability cases during the sue-crazy times of the 1970s and 1980s, Sturm, Ruger pistols made after 1977 have roll marking on the barrels with the following legend: "BEFORE USING GUN—READ WARNINGS IN INSTRUCTION MANUAL AVAILABLE FREE FROM STURM, RUGER & COMPANY, INC., SOUTHPORT, CT., U.S.A." (Other versions of the company's pistols and other firearms made after that date also have such a warning.) The position occupied by the roll marking was originally used for the "Sturm, Ruger & Company" trademark.

This Mark I version of the Ruger pistol is a post-1971 "New Model" version since its emblem is on the right grip panel. (Photo courtesy of Sturm, Ruger and Company.)

Shown is the left side of the "New Model" Mark I pistol. Like the Standard pistols, these had a "silver" trigger and magazine base. (Photo courtesy of Sturm, Ruger and Company.)

All Mark I pistols (as well as Standard versions) also have "Made in the 200th Year of American Liberty" stamped on them if they were made during the U.S. Bicentennial in 1976.

Both the Standard and Mark I were sold with magazines that did not have a Ruger falcon emblem on the base (a silver and black falcon is to be found on the end plate of the Mark II series magazines). Old Model magazines have the follower button on the right while New Model magazines (designated AMC magazine) have the follower on the left (or reversed to the right for use in Old Model guns). Capacity of both Old Model and New Model magazines is nine rounds.

The Mark I AMC magazine (right) has a silver base which does not have a Ruger falcon. The new M-10 magazine (left), designed for the Mark II series, is easier to reload and disassemble for cleaning. (Photo courtesy of Sturm, Ruger and Company.)

The Mark I Short Barrel

Catalog number T514, this model was made only from 1952 to 1953. This pistol had a 5 1/4-inch tapered barrel and target sights; the front sight was not as sharply undercut as the T678 or bull barrel models that were to follow. All these pistols had the black falcon emblem only on left grip plates. Even though the pistol was hailed by writers as the perfect addition to the Ruger lineup, demand for the pistol was such that it was discontinued. It has now become one of the harder-to-obtain collector's guns.

The Mark I 5¼-inch-barrel version of the Ruger pistol was only available for a short time. (Photo courtesy of Sturm, Ruger and Company.)

The Mark I Bull Barrel

This model, catalog number T512, was introduced in 1964. The pistol had a nontapering, 5 1/2-inch barrel with a front sight base attached by screws to the top of the barrel. The rear target sight and other features are the same as that of the Mark I pistols. In 1969, the Micro sight on the Mark I Bull Barrel (as well as other Mark I models) was replaced with an unmarked sight.

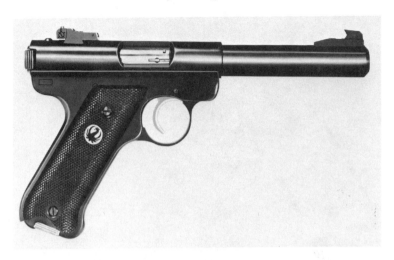

The Mark I Bull Barrel, introduced in 1964, has a nontapering 5½-inch barrel with a front sight base attached by screws to the top of the barrel. The right view of the pistol is shown. (Photo courtesy of Sturm, Ruger and Company.)

The left side of the Mark I Bull Barrel, catalog number T512, is shown here. The rear target sight and many other features are the same as those of the Mark I pistols. (Photo courtesy of Sturm, Ruger and Company.)

The "Millionth Standard" was a one-of-a-kind pistol, marking the production of one million of the Standard guns by Sturm, Ruger and Company during the company's thirtieth anniversary in 1979. Pictured is the right view of the pistol. (Photo courtesy of Sturm, Ruger and Company.)

Shown is the left view of the Ruger "Millionth Standard." Roll marks are highlighted by gold inlay, and the ivory grips each have a red falcon emblem. (Photo courtesy of Sturm, Ruger and Company.)

The "Millionth Standard"

A one-of-a-kind gun, this pistol marked the production of one million of the Standard pistols by Sturm, Ruger & Company during the company's thirtieth anniversary in 1979.

The blued-steel pistol has a 4 3/4-inch barrel and is covered with intricate floral engraving (done by Ray Viramontez). It also has ivory grip plates (provided by Bob Purdy and hand carved by Ron Lang) with a red falcon emblem rather than the standard black. The bolt is machine-jeweled with gold inlay highlighting some of the engraving as well as the standard roll marks, William Ruger's signature on the right side of the barrel, the "1000000" serial number, and the Ruger falcon trademark placed at the top of the receiver with "1949-1979" at its base.

The pistol was encased in a velvet-lined, glass-topped walnut box which bore an engraved silver plate on its lid. The pistol was purchased for $27,200 by Austin M. Wortley, Jr., in a sealed-bid auction. Proceeds from the sale went to the United States Shooting Team and the 1980 U.S. Olympic Shooting Team. The auction was handled by Stoy, Malone & Company of Bethesda, MD.

Limited Run of Standard Pistols

The final limited run of five thousand Standard pistols with 4 3/4-inch barrels was made in January 1982. These were collector's pistols and bore Ruger's signature over the top of the receiver along with the notation, "1 of 5000" on the right side of the barrel. The pistols were made of stainless steel and had the original red falcon emblem on the right grips. Each pistol also had a wooden "salt-cod"-style box made for it since such boxes were used to mail the original pistols to customers.

(Interestingly enough, Sturm, Ruger produced press release photos of the stainless steel guns without the "1 of 5000" roll marking on the barrel, suggesting that the company might have had plans to sell stainless steel Standard pistols. But actual production of the gun, other than the collector's series, was never carried out.)

The final limited run of five thousand stainless steel, collectors' Standard pistols with 4¾-inch barrels was made in January 1982. (Photo courtesy of Sturm, Ruger and Company.)

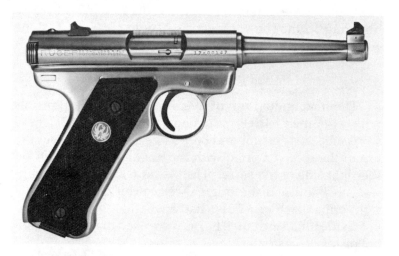

A stainless steel Standard gun without the "1 of 5000" roll marking on the barrel is shown. The serial number and red medallion on the grip panel suggest the "1 of 5000" caption was airbrushed off this photo by a company artist. (Photo courtesy of Sturm, Ruger and Company.)

The left side of the stainless steel Standard shows the Ruger signature roll mark missing from the pistol. The photo suggests Ruger might have had plans to sell stainless Standards at one point before the Mark II series was introduced. (Photo courtesy of Sturm, Ruger and Company.)

The Mark II Standard

Introduced along with the other Mark II models in 1982, the Standard, like other Mark IIs, is most readily distinguishable from the original Standard by the addition of a bolt stop on the left side of the pistol just above the left pistol grip. All the variants in the Mark II series also have a new, easier-to-insert magazine (designated the M-10) with 10-round capacity, a slightly modified trigger made by a new manufacturing method so that it fits the pistol more precisely, a grooved trigger pivot that is retained by a musical wire spring (rather than a C-clip), a safety that could be activated before the pistol is cocked and loaded, shallow scallops cut into the rear of the receiver tube for easier grasping of the bolt ears, and a larger diameter magazine latch that is easier to operate, holds the magazine more securely, and minimizes the gap between the frame and latch to help keep out dirt.

As with the original Standard and all other variants of the Ruger pistol, the barrels are tightly attached to the re-

Shown is the left view of the Mark II Standard (MK-4). The new magazine has a black base rather than the "silver" of the original. While the trigger pull is much smoother and better than the original, the "silver" finish has been retained. (Photo courtesy of Sturm, Ruger and Company.)

While the Mark II Standard (MK-4) pistol in blued steel with a 4¾-inch barrel is very similar to the original Ruger pistol, continued improvements make it even more reliable and durable. Shown is the right view. (Photo courtesy of Sturm, Ruger and Company.)

The Mark II Standard blued pistol (MK-4) is shown with the bolt locked open. The bolt can be closed by pushing down on the release at the top of the grip panel or, when having a loaded magazine, by pulling on the bolt "ears." (Photo courtesy of Sturm, Ruger and Company.)

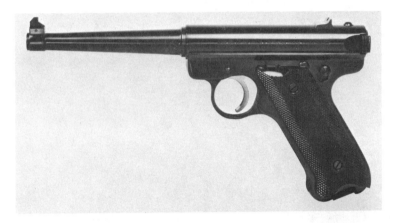

Like other Mark II guns, the Mark II Standard blued pistol (MK-6) with 6-inch barrel has an improved trigger, a bolt hold-open mechanism, and a better safety. (Photo courtesy of Sturm, Ruger and Company.)

ceiver with 20-pitch threading. Many parts in the old Standard and new Mark II Standard guns are interchangeable, but the magazines are not. Old magazines are readily distinguishable by the silver base, which does not have a Ruger falcon on it; the new M-10 magazines have a round, spiral spring in the front, while the old AMC magazines have a wide, squared-coil spring that fills the interior of the magazine and is readily seen through the follower button slot.

In addition to the blued models, stainless steel models were added to the Mark II Standard company's lineup in 1984. The use of stainless steel is denoted by a "K" in catalog-number prefixes.

There are four models of the Mark II Standard: the MK-4 (4 3/4-inch barrel), MK-6 (6-inch barrel), KMK-4 (stainless steel, 4 3/4-inch barrel), and KMK-6 (stainless steel, 6-inch barrel). All have square-notch, fixed rear sights that are dovetailed into the top of the rear receiver tube. The front sight is of the original Standard style, Partridge type and 0.093 inches wide; it is held in place by a pin and barrel band.

Pictured is the right view of the Mark II Standard (KMK-4) pistol in stainless steel with a 4¾-inch barrel. Note Ruger's artistic touch, which is created by having the trigger, grips, magazine base, and sights a contrasting black. (Photo courtesy of Sturm, Ruger and Company.)

Barrels are tapered (as with the original Standard models) and have the 1-in-14 twist found with all other Mark II versions (except for the Government Model). Delrin plastic grips have a silver-falcon-on-black-background emblem on the right grip with sharp checkering on both grips.

The beveled rear receiver of the Mark II Standard KMK-4 makes bolt "ears" even easier to grasp when cocking the pistol, which is shown from the left view. (Photo courtesy of Sturm, Ruger and Company.)

The Mark II Standard Model with a 6-inch barrel (KMK-6) is made of stainless steel and has the overall layout of other Mark II pistols. (Photo courtesy of Sturm, Ruger and Company.)

The Mark II Target Model

Available in blued steel (as the MK-678) or—in post-1984 guns—stainless steel (as the KMK-678), this pistol has a tapered, button-rifled barrel that is 6 7/8 inches long. The front sight is 0.125 inches wide with a sharp undercut to reduce glare; the rear sight is click-adjustable for both windage and elevation.

Like the Mark II Standard and Mark II Bull Barrels, the stainless steel guns reflect Ruger's artistic tastes as well as good design standards; each stainless gun's trigger is "blued" (blued guns have "silver" triggers), grips are black, and the front and rear sights are the standard blued steel. This gives the guns a very pleasing look and has a practical side as well, since the blued front and rear sight create a much better sight picture than do stainless steel sights (several other manufacturers would do well to learn this).

Barrels of the Mark II Target are tapered. Like others in the Mark II series, the Target models have a 1-in-14 twist barrel, Delrin plastic grips with sharp checkering, and the black falcon emblem on the right grip.

In 1984, Ruger introduced the Mark II Target Model in stainless steel, known as the KMK-678. Like other Ruger target guns, the rear sight is click-adjustable for both windage and elevation. (Photo courtesy of Sturm, Ruger and Company.)

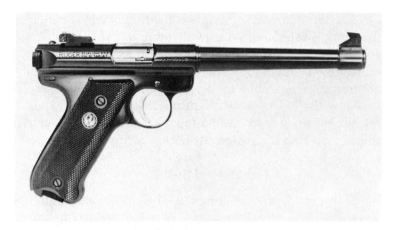

The blued-steel Mark II Target Model (MK-678) has a tapered, button-rifled barrel that is 6⅞ inches long. The front sight has a sharp undercut to reduce glare. (Photo courtesy of Sturm, Ruger and Company.)

The Mark II Target pistol (MK-678) has a tapered, 1-in-14 twist barrel and Delrin plastic grips with sharp checkering. The pistol is shown here from its left side. Accuracy is better than with pistols costing twice as much. (Photo courtesy of Sturm, Ruger and Company.)

The Target models (as well as the Bull Barrel versions of the Mark II listed below) are very accurate and are inexpensive—costing only about half as much as any other pistol with similar capabilities. Most target shooters using quality ammunition are able to average sub-inch groups at 25 yards, with "high velocity" ammunition normally expanding the group size by only a fourth of an inch at 25 yards, thereby making the pistols ideal for hunting needs as well.

The Mark II Bull Barrel

These models were introduced in 1982 with stainless steel versions and a 10-inch bull barrel added to the line in 1984. The 6 7/8-inch barrel, blued Government Model was added in 1987. As the name suggests, all have a heavy bull barrel in 5 1/2- (catalog number MK-512), 6 7/8- (MK-678-G), or 10-inch lengths (MK-10) in the blued models and 5 1/2 or 10 inches in stainless steel ("K" prefix for KMK-512 and KMK-10). It would seem probable that a 6 7/8 stainless steel KMK-678-G version will be offered in the near future.

The Mark II Bull Barrel model was introduced in 1982. The 5½-inch barrel gives the pistol a forward balance, which is desired by many target shooters, and the added mass helps reduce recoil. (Photo courtesy of Sturm, Ruger and Company.)

Here we see the right side of the Mark II Bull Barrel (MK-512). Skilled shooters using quality ammunition are able to shoot sub-1-inch groups at 25 yards with these (and other) Ruger pistols. (Photo courtesy of Sturm, Ruger and Company.)

The Mark II Bull Barrel in stainless steel was added to the Ruger line in 1984. The pistol has a 5½-inch, heavy bull barrel (catalog number MK512). The pistol is shown from the left view. (Photo courtesy of Sturm, Ruger and Company.)

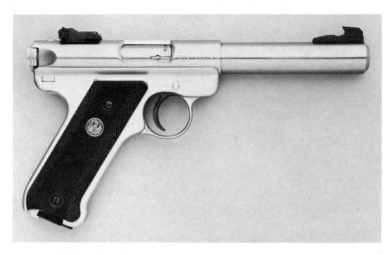

Seen from the right, the stainless steel Mark II Bull Barrel (MK-512) has a rear sight, trigger, and grips like those found on other Mark II pistols; the front sight base, however, is slightly different. (Photo courtesy of Sturm, Ruger and Company.)

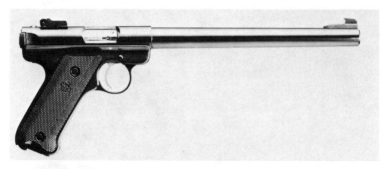

The Mark II Bull Barrel (MK-10) was added to the Ruger line in 1984. This gun's serial number, XLA-4, suggests it was an experimental prototype. (Photo courtesy of Sturm, Ruger and Company.)

The 5 1/2-inch bull barrel is nontapered, but the other longer barrels have a very slight taper to them. The rear sight, trigger, and grips are like those of the other Mark II pistols. The front sight is slightly different and has its sight base attached by a screw to the top of the barrel rather than attached by a barrel band.

The Mark II Bull Barrel (MK-10) is heavy but accurate. The heavy barrel is sometimes mistaken for a silencer, causing no end of confusion among the ill-informed. (Photo courtesy of Sturm, Ruger and Company.)

Made of stainless steel, the Mark II Bull Barrel KMK-10 sports a 10-inch bull barrel. Most .22 LR ammunition achieves maximum velocity in a barrel this long. (Photo courtesy of Sturm, Ruger and Company.)

All of these pistols are very accurate. Most accurate of the family is the Government Model (MK-678-G), which is the blued, 6 7/8-inch barrel version in this series. It is identical to the new guns being sold to the U.S. military and has a 1-in-15 twist rather than the 1-in-16 found in other Mark II versions.

The most accurate of the Ruger family of pistols is the Government Model (MK-678-G). It is identical to the gun sold to the U.S. military and has a 1-in-15 twist. (Photo courtesy of Sturm, Ruger and Company.)

The Government Model was originally created according to U.S. military specifications and received very favorable publicity after being chosen by the military. It has been purchased from Sturm, Ruger & Company to replace the earlier Mark Is and the pistols of other manufacturers that were previously used for match target pistols and as training guns. Once the pistol was put into production, Ruger decided to introduce a version of the gun to the public as well. Civilian models have "Government Target Model" roll-marked on the rear right side of the receiver; those sold to the military read "U.S." over the serial number on the right front of the receiver.

Both versions of the Government Model are targeted at the factory with a laser-sighting system to assure accuracy, and the factory-test target is included with the pistol to show its potential accuracy (with most groups being well within the one-inch maximum range called for by the military).

It is interesting to note that government tests of these

pistols have found that they will fire ten thousand rounds without any parts breakage or any measurable wear; this certainly spotlights the good design, quality control, and ruggedness of all the Ruger pistols.

Strangely enough, even though the U.S. military found that the Ruger pistols outperformed all others available, more expensive pistols are often found in civilian target-shooting contests and—more often than not—the Rugers used there have seen a lot of custom gunsmithing work and have had their barrels replaced by the "target" barrels of other companies. One well-known gun expert (who asked not to be named) suggested that, more than anything else, this was due to the "snob value" of the more expensive and exotic guns. And when it comes to snob value, the lower price tag of the Ruger gun has actually worked against it among many members of the shooting elite.

In fact, with a little "tuning" of the trigger and perhaps the replacement of the rear sights by more sensitive sights (or even just the screws by those with extra "click" notches), the Government Model will probably shoot as well or better than anything else on the market. It would seem probable that, in the near future, this will cause the "snob" guns to fall to the wayside in shooting contests. Snob value isn't greater than winning.

At any rate, in its recent independent test of the Government Model, *American Rifleman* found that, when fired from a rest, it was capable occasionally of groups as small as 0.18 inches with Federal Champion ammunition, with average groups for several types of target ammunition ranging from 0.41 to 0.69 inches at 25 yards. Such tests leave little doubt that the Government Model is capable of better accuracy than most shooters can ever realize.

Sturm, Ruger .22 Automatic Pistol Specifications

Name	Length (in.)	Weight (Unloaded) (oz.)	Barrel Length (in.)	Sights
RST4	8 3/4	36	4 3/4	Fixed
RST6	10	38	6	Fixed

Sturm, Ruger .22 Automatic Pistol Specifications

Name	Length (in.)	Weight (Unloaded) (oz.)	Barrel Length (in.)	Sights
T678	10 7/8	42	6 7/8	Target
T514	9 1/4	39	5 1/4	Target
T512	9 1/2	42	5 1/2	Target
MK-4	8 5/16	36	4 3/4	Fixed
MK-6	10 5/16	38	6	Fixed
KMK-4	8 5/16	36	4 3/4	Fixed
KMK-6	10 5/16	38	6	Fixed
MK-678	11 1/8	42	6 7/8	Target
KMK-678	11 1/8	42	6 7/8	Target
MK-512	9 13/16	42	5 1/2	Target
MK-678 G	11 1/8	46	6 7/8	Target
MK-10	14 1/4	52	10	Target
KMK-512	9 13/16	42	5 1/2	Target
KMK-10	14 1/4	52	10	Target

CUSTOMIZED VERSIONS
OF THE RUGER .22 PISTOLS

A number of gunsmiths and tinkers have made minor or even major modifications to the Ruger pistols in order to make them more suitable to individual needs. Most of these modifications consist of smoothing out and/or reducing the pull and overtravel of the trigger and may include replacing the barrel and pistol grips.

Care should be taken with any Ruger pistol that has been altered with a new barrel designed for target work, since some have chambers cut for slightly less than the SAAMI maximum case dimensions. Trying to chamber a shell like the CCI Stinger with a case that won't take maximum shells could risk a slam-firing of the cartridge, especially if some fouling is present. Such an event is rare, but brass fragments and powder residue might cause some injuries, and the bullet might end up jammed in the barrel or headed in an undesirable direction during such an event. So, a little caution is in order.

One of the first gunsmiths to carry out custom work on Ruger pistols was Carl J. Davis, who described some of his work in the September 1964 issue of *American Rifleman*. In addition to rebarreling and modifying pistols for the .22 LR, he also reworked some of the Ruger guns to fire the .22 Short. The major part of this adaptation consisted of using a High Standard Olympic magazine with the pistol and replacing the barrel with a 1-in-24 twist Douglas barrel chambered for the .22 Short. The barrel had a 12-degree forcing cone and the barrel ramp, Davis found, was not necessary, since the High Standard magazine had an integral feed ramp of its own.

Davis had special rounded grips with finger rests on some of his modified pistols and an aluminum ramp occasionally over the barrel. In addition to standard Mark I sights, Smith & Wesson and Elliason rear sights were used, and the front sight was replaced by National Match 1911 sights when necessary. Because of the reduced recoil of the .22 Short, the spring of the Ruger had to be shortened and the bolt greatly lightened by milling cuts in its rear sides and top. Davis pistols also often have set screws in the lower side of the trigger guard to take up slack and overtravel screws in the trigger itself.

Another pistolsmith doing a lot of similar work was competition shooter Jim Clark of Shreveport, Louisiana. The work done varied from pistol to pistol, but his work generally consisted of replacing the barrel with a heavy Douglas barrel (of varying lengths from gun to gun) with a 1-in-14 twist and—occasionally—an integral muzzle brake created by two milling cuts toward the muzzle end of the barrel. Clark often replaced the trigger with one of his own design that had a wide serrated trigger (with an overtravel stop).

Many of Clark's guns have replacement sights, which were put on by Clark himself (or the gun's owner). Rear sights found on the Clark-modified pistols include those designed by George Elliason, John E. Giles, or Clark himself. Often a new, longer follower was placed in standard magazines to hold the bolt open after the last shot had been fired.

John E. Giles also did some customizing work on competition pistols. Most of his pistols sport Douglas barrels and sights designed by Giles. Some had extended-rib front sights and Herrett custom grips.

Mag-Na-Port Arms also produced a limited number of customized Rugers for the collector's market. These were created by engraving Mark II 5 1/2-inch Bull Barrel pistols and adding the company's muzzle-compensating cuts on either side of the front sight. This type of modified pistol was sold as the "Stalker."

At the time of this writing, Tom Volquartsen is doing beautiful custom work on Ruger pistols; guns are available in a number of "packaged" configurations as well as custom work done to the buyer's specifications. Conversions are based around the replacement of the barrel by any of a number of Douglas barrels chambered and reworked by Volquartsen, replacement of the rear sight with one made by Bo-Mar or Millet, replacement of the front sight with one of Volquartsen's design, use of barrel compensators, and choice of various grips: Pachmayr, hand-made grips by Bowlers (of England), or those designed by Volquartsen himself.

Internally, Volquartsen also tunes the action for a lighter pull and reduced overtravel, often jeweling the bolt and trigger. A choice of finishes is available to the shooter, including nickel plating and Teflon.

In addition to having modification packages done to a customer's own pistol, Volquartsen also sells "pre-customized" guns. The gunsmith has shown a flair for romantic names for his package custom work, with the modified guns sporting such names as "The Terminator" (a sightless model with integral scope mounts for use with a pistol scope, Aimpoint, or Armson OEG), "The Predator," "The Olympic," and "The Masters." More "mundane" names include "The Supreme" and "The Deluxe." By whatever name, the work is good and prices are reasonable. Best of all, a customer can have just a little work done to his own firearm if he finds the basic fit and feel of the regular Ruger pistol to his liking.

AMT LIGHTNING

The Lightning pistol is a copy of the Ruger .22 automatic and has only a few cosmetic differences (such as a more squared-off receiver and a spike on the front of the trigger guard), making it visibly different from the Ruger pistols. Magazines and pistol grips designed for the Ruger pistols will work with the Lightning, generally without modification.

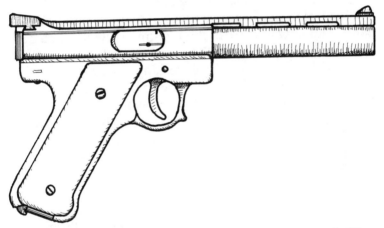

The AMT Lightning Bullseye model has a ventilated rib over a bull barrel and wooden grips. While the AMT gun has slab sides and a hook in the trigger guard, the design is purely that of Ruger, having been "borrowed" since the inventor's patent rights have expired.

Like the Ruger, the Lightning points well and is quite accurate for a .22 pistol. The AMT Lightning is available in a number of barrel lengths; 6 1/2-, 8 1/2-, 10-, and 12 1/2-inch standard and bull barrel styles are available (along with a 5-inch bull barrel). AMT also markets a 6 1/2-inch barrel Bullseye model, with a ventilated rib over a bull barrel and wooden grips being standard features.

Although the longer barrels available for the Lightning are somewhat awkward to use, they do offer maximum velocity with most .22 ammunition (which gains maximum velocity at around 8 to 10 inches of barrel length) and can quiet down the report of a .22 LR considerably, especially if special ammunition like .22 CB Long Caps is used. The longer sighting radius of such guns might also help somewhat with accuracy for some shooters.

The Lightning's scope-mount cuts in its upper receiver allow for the easy mounting of a pistol scope. Adjustable target sights are available for an additional cost on all models. Wrap-around Pachmayr grips are standard on the pistols, as are Clark adjustable triggers.

AMT also made a one thousand-run, limited edition Baby Auto Mag version of the Lightning which had a high ventilated rib over an 8 1/2-inch barrel, adjustable sights, and a wider-than-normal bolt cocking cut area. This pistol was designed to look like the .44 Auto Mag that AMT manufactured for a short time and that appeared in one of Clint Eastwood's "Dirty Harry" movies; as such, a few special serial numbers were roll-marked with "Make My Day" and "Feel Lucky Punk."

The Lightning is a good pistol, but it does carry a bit higher price tag than the Ruger pistols. This factor often makes it a second choice for many would-be buyers. Many shooters also feel that the functioning and fit of the Ruger pistols is better, though the Lightning is certainly well made and dependable by any standards.

Before the Lightning was first introduced, AMT marketed a line of receiver/barrel assemblies that will fit on the Ruger pistols (as well as the Lightning). Demand apparently wasn't too great for these as they are no longer offered as separate accessories for the Ruger or Lightning pistols.

MACHINE PISTOL VERSIONS OF THE RUGER

Before the manufacture of automatic weapons for anyone other than government agencies was banned in the United States late in 1987, it was possible legally to convert the Ruger pistol to selective-fire operation in many states.

Because the Ruger pistol functions very reliably, these conversions work well, though the gun's light bolt makes cycling quite rapid; it is therefore hard to fire less than a magazine's worth of ammunition with one trigger pull.

One excellent conversion for the Ruger pistol is detailed in the book, *The Ruger Pistol Exotic Weapons System*, available from Paladin Press (see Appendix B). The conversion described in the book makes use of a trip-firing mechanism to release the sear when the bolt comes forward and chambers a round. Though many readers cannot make such conversions legally, the book is of great interest to many Ruger pistol fans. It also has a wealth of ideas regarding muzzle brakes, forward pistol grips (mounted to the front of the frame or below the barrel), barrel shrouds, and rifle-style stocks that can easily be carried out with little or no machining work.

Selective-fire conversion for the Ruger pistol as outlined in *The Ruger Pistol Exotic Weapons System*. The conversion described in the book makes use of a trip-firing mechanism to release the sear when the bolt comes forward and chambers a round.

Given the lethality of multiple hits of .22 bullets and the worldwide availability of the ammunition, one has to wonder whether the military or police officer of the future might not be found with a weapon very similar to a selective-fire Ruger pistol. At any rate, though rare, a few selective-fire Ruger pistols have been made and are occasionally seen for legal sale to individuals who can meet federal, state, and local laws restricting their ownership.

"CARBINE" VERSIONS OF THE RUGER PISTOL

Carbine versions of the Ruger .22 pistol are very rarely ever encountered—if at all.

The reason for this isn't because of legalities. Because of the way federal firearms laws are written, rifles can be cut down to pistol configurations only with special permission and a lot of red tape. Pistols, however, can be legally altered to rifle size without any paperwork, provided they meet the minimum dimensions of a 16-inch or longer barrel and an overall length of 26 inches or more (local or state regulations differ from federal law, so it's wise to check before launching into a do-it-yourself carbine project).

Pistols converted to carbines either on a custom basis or even by gun manufacturers were the vogue at the beginning of the 1900s. Lugers, "Broomhandle" Mausers, Colt 1911s, Browning Hi-Powers, and revolvers were found with stocks on them; even a few modern pistols, such as the Beretta 93 and Heckler & Koch VP70 are to be seen with such devices. But the modern two-hand holds (as opposed to the single-hand grip of the past), along with prone shooting and the use of tree limbs or the like to steady the firearm (and good old-fashioned practice), have proven that it's possible to keep a standard pistol steady enough to actually get the same accuracy as a stocked gun.

While a Ruger "Carbine" is technically possible, few, if any, are ever seen. In the hands of a skilled shooter using a two-hand hold or rest, the pistol is nearly as accurate as and considerably less awkward to carry than a carbine.

So, while a stock may improve control with selective-fire pistols or help the novice score hits earlier in training, a stock on a pistol in the hands of a skilled shooter does little to improve his shooting and adds enough bulk and length to make it as bulky as—well, a carbine.

The list of drawbacks doesn't end there: The bullet's muzzle velocity increase realized from a 16-inch barrel won't be much greater than from a 6-inch Standard barrel and may even be the same or less than that imparted by a 10-inch pistol. There are excellent, lightweight, low-priced .22 rifles such as Ruger's 10/22 that are readily available. And there is that recoiling bolt that is just inches away from the shooter's nose during the recoil cycle; not dangerous if the face is kept back, but disconcerting, nevertheless. There are wire stocks that a shooter can hold on the pistol if he needs a cheek support and wants to shoot from the shoulder without making any alterations to his pistol.

So, given all these considerations, why pay custom-work prices when you can buy an excellent rifle like the 10/22 for less money? Little wonder a carbine version of a Ruger pistol is seldom seen, if ever, since it's more or less a losing proposition for most shooters.

Altering a Ruger pistol to a carbine in itself would be a fairly straightforward task for a skilled gunsmith. The barrel needs to be replaced by a longer one or—possibly—a "flash hider" welded to the barrel to give it a 16-inch length. Securing a stock to the pistol would be a bit trickier since it must be attached somehow to the pistol grip; generally a detachable Mauser-style stock would be most practical though this would depend on the customizer's whims. A number of other possibilities exist, including a detachable stock/barrel extension that would make a pistol "legal" when in its rifle configuration while allowing the shooter to quickly convert it back to its pistol incarnation.

For most shooters, the Ruger pistol/carbine is a possibility that just isn't worth realizing.

****

Regardless of which Ruger pistol a shooter buys, it is probable that with a little care, it will give its owner a lot of shooting for his money.

As mentioned above, government tests of these pistols have found that they will fire ten thousand rounds without any parts breakage or any measurable wear; independent laboratory tests have taken this number to 41,000 rounds without any malfunctions or measurable wear. (And the author has heard of pistols with the numbers of rounds through them without parts breakage given in the millions. While such numbers are a bit too good to be believed, the fact that such stories are told at all and are not challenged at the time of the telling shows just how much faith consumers have come to have in the Ruger pistols.)

Such tests and tales certainly spotlight the good design, quality control, and ruggedness of all the Ruger pistols. Since most shooters never put anywhere near 41,000 rounds through their pistols, guns that are properly cared for will probably become heirlooms.

Chapter 3

Care and Maintenance

With proper care, the useful life of the Sturm, Ruger pistol can be greatly extended; abuse or careless cleaning techniques can quickly spoil or even ruin the firearm. With a little tender loving care, a Ruger pistol can easily last a lifetime and even be used by one's children and grandchildren.

About the only special tools needed for maintaining a Ruger pistol (other than those normally found in most home shops) are special gunsmithing screwdrivers to remove the only two screws used on the Standard gun to fasten on its grips. Owners of Mark I or Mark II Target or Bull Barrel versions will also need two very small screwdrivers with different sized blades to adjust the rear sights screws if the screws are to remain unburred.

CLEANING

The first order of business when cleaning a firearm or doing any work on one is to be sure it's unloaded. (No end of people are shot every year because they start cleaning an "empty" firearm that turns out to be loaded.) The same goes for casually inspecting a firearm; always check to be sure it's unloaded unless you're about to shoot it.

The accuracy of a Ruger .22 pistol can be ruined by improper cleaning; it's better not to clean a pistol's bore at all rather than to do a halfway job of it. There is some truth to the old wives' tale that .22 firearms should never be cleaned; those who proceed to clean a pistol improperly can cause wear to the gun's barrel and make it less accurate and reliable than if it were never cleaned. Now that corrosive primers aren't being used on quality ammunition, the need to clean it after every shooting session is uncalled for except for anyone concerned about milking the last bit of accuracy from his Ruger.

Since the muzzle is the last part of the gun to touch a bullet as it thunders out of the pistol, it makes sense that any damage to this end of things can quickly ruin accuracy. Consequently, the main consideration when cleaning a pistol is to take care not to damage the muzzle by rubbing or binding against its bore with a cleaning rod.

Ideally, a Ruger pistol barrel is cleaned by pushing or pulling cleaning brush and patches through the gun from the breech to the muzzle. This is practical, since field-stripping removes the bolt, and the rear of the receiver is open to allow a cleaning rod to be inserted. So (for those who haven't got the drift of things), don't clean from the muzzle end of the gun.

Take your time while cleaning a pistol if the gun is to remain undamaged and reliable. Cleaning patches and the brush should move from the chamber to the muzzle so that dirt is pushed in one direction only; going back and forth with brush and patches just shoves the fouling up and down the bore without working all of it out of the gun.

Aluminum cleaning rods are better than nothing if kept free of grit. They can become like files if they pick up a bit of sand or metal, quickly eating into the pistol's bore. Consequently, care must be taken to religiously keep an aluminum cleaning rod free of grit. Another problem is that quite a bit of pressure is needed to push a tight patch through a bore; unfortunately, aluminum rods have a terrible habit of bending.

Steel cleaning rods are a better bet. Many find a U.S.

military surplus, steel cleaning rod ideal, especially if cleaning must be done outside, since the steel rod is less apt to bend or pick up grit. The brush and patches made for the M16 (AR-15) rifle will work well in the .22 pistol.

Those wanting to maintain the maximum accuracy of a Target or Bull Barrel model of the Ruger pistol should invest in a plastic-coated, steel cleaning rod. They're a little hard to find (one good one is made by Parker-Hale and can be ordered through most gun shops). However, the plastic coating will pick up grit; care must therefore be taken, and it should never be used in the field. If kept free of grit, the coating does give maximum protection to the pistol's bore during cleaning.

In addition to the military-surplus patches designed for the M16 rifle, it is also possible to purchase a jag (a pointed rod that goes on the cleaning rod) and use it to push paper towels through the bore; many pistol owners prefer to do so since they can get a very tight fit and the paper is cheap to use and almost always available. Another tool that can prove useful is an old toothbrush that can reach inside the receiver; it can be used to scrub the bolt.

Break-Free CLP is the first choice as a lubricant/cleaner for firearms. This liquid was created for U.S. military firearms, and it works over a wide temperature range. It is made to both clean and lubricate so that bore cleaning fluid is no longer needed. Once on the pistol, it will continue to work so that, hours later, dirt can often be wiped off a gun having a bit of Break-Free CLP on it.

Another lubricant and cleaner that has recently become available and that rivals the abilities of Break-Free CLP is Outers' new Tri-Lube. It too works to clean and lubricate guns and helps prevent rust once in place on the pistol. Tri-Lube's real plus is that it can work in temperatures ranging from −65°F to 475°F. This makes it ideal for areas where the temperature frequently drops below zero.

Because Break-Free CLP or Tri-Lube take time for their silicon lubricants to set up, allow the Ruger pistol to sit for half an hour or so after applying the fluid for full lubrication before firing. (It should be noted that both Break-Free CLP and military-surplus cleaning kits with steel rods are available from such military-surplus companies as Sierra Supply and Sherwood International. Tri-Lube is readily available at most gun shops.)

Break-Free CLP or Tri-Lube should not be used to clean the magazine or allowed to touch .22 ammunition. They should not be left in the chamber of a pistol as they will quickly deactivate any .22 ammunition they touch because they are penetrating oils. When cleaning the magazine, a soft brush and a powder fouling solvent would be a good bet; be sure to clean any oil out of the chamber with a dry patch when cleaning is completed.

A *very light* coat of oil on steel parts will help prevent rust. After the pistol has been cleaned, the bore should be checked to be sure it is clear of patch threads and oil. Any material left in the barrel can ruin it with the firing of just one shot. Avoid getting oil on wooden pistol grips, as it can gradually stain the wood or even damage it.

With stainless steel versions of the Ruger pistol, lubrication is also essential to prevent wear and tear on parts. Stainless steel guns cannot be fired "dry" without excessive wear. Also, "stainless" steel isn't as stainless as many think; it is really corrosion-resistant, not stainless, and a little lubricant is necessary for its protection. (As an alternative to oil to protect the pistol's finish, some users put a coat of paste wax designed for use on metal on the outside of the pistol. They allow it to dry and then buff it. This works well if the paste wax is replaced from time to time.)

Oil should be used sparingly on internal parts since thick coats of oil don't improve lubricating properties and may actually gum things up as dirt becomes trapped in the oil. Too much oil will actually increase the wear and tear on the Ruger pistol. Also, avoid oils like WD-40 or others designed for electrical motors and the like, since they have a tendency to gunk up over time and may not give much protection from rust.

When cleaning a pistol, a degreasing solvent (or alcohol

or acetone/nail-polish remover if you're in a rush) can sometimes be of great use in cleaning out the crud that can accumulate inside a pistol that's been carried around for a while.

Bore cleaning is normally carried out by starting with a brush on the cleaning rod. Those using Break-Free or Tri-Lube will use this solvent/lubricant throughout the cleaning process; those using a solvent and oil will start with the solvent on the brush at this point. It may take a number of scrubbings with the brush to get the fouling loosened up. Plan to spend more cleaning time after a long shooting session than when just a few shots have been fired from the pistol.

Once the brush has been used, the shooter should then push some very tight, dry patches through the bore from the breech and out the muzzle. At this point, the bore will look clean and, if only a little shooting has been done, it is pretty clean. But to get it really clean, it's a good idea to push a patch soaked in Break-Free or Tri-Lube (or solvent) from the chamber and out the muzzle so that the bore is liberally coated with the solvent. That done, the bore should be left for at least half an hour (with a couple of hours more desirable).

That done, use the wire-brush tip on the cleaning rod and then push very tight patches through the bore, alternating between patches soaked in Break-Free or Tri-Lube and dry patches. Keep doing this until the patches start coming out clean. Once clean, a dry patch should be run through the bore if shooting will take place soon; if the pistol is to remain in storage or in a holster for some time, push a patch lightly lubricated with Break-Free through the bore before quitting.

Be sure to clean the bolt (especially the bolt face) and recoil spring of the Ruger pistol thoroughly with a toothbrush soaked with Break-Free or Tri-Lube before reassembling the gun. Also take care to clean the small groove in the chamber end of the barrel where the extractor fits (a wooden toothpick may help here).

In extremely cold weather or dusty conditions, non-oil silicon lubricants or similar products can help keep the Ruger pistol functioning better than many gun oils. One good choice for such use is E & L Manufacturing's Gun Lube.

If it's necessary to store a pistol for several months or more, be sure the firearm is not placed in a leather or nylon holster or an airtight gun rug. Leather generally attracts moisture and often contains acids that will attack the metal of the gun with time; many nylon holsters and gun rugs are knit tightly enough to also allow moisture to condense inside them—with disastrous results. Don't store guns in airtight plastic bags or vinyl sacks; these, too, will rust a firearm, since moisture will condense inside them when the temperature varies even a few degrees.

On blued-steel models of the Ruger pistol, touch-up blue is useful for darkening down edges when the bluing has worn off due to holster wear or nicks or scratches on the finish of the firearm. Touch-up blue can also spruce up a gun if it is to be sold.

Minor rust spots can be removed from blued areas with fine steel wool and oil, and the surface refinished with touch-up blue (after first removing the oil with acetone or alcohol). On stainless steel guns, light discoloration can be removed with a rubber eraser or metal-polishing compounds. Care should be taken to rub in the direction of buffing marks on the pistol's surface so that the new work will blend into the pistol's finish.

Major rust spots that pit into the finish are often a job for a gunsmith, though some do-it-yourselfers may be able to tackle heavy rust spots with a Dremel tool with a fine wire brush. But care has to be used so that the brush doesn't dig down into the pistol's finish.

Follow the directions on the bottle of touch-up blue, as directions vary from manufacturer to manufacturer. Touch-up blue does not cover major scratches or large flat patches very well, but it does work well in touching up light wear and tear or rust spots. Be sure, too, to clean and oil the area where touch-up blue has been used, since some types can promote rust after the chemical is used.

In areas where high humidity promotes rust, Outers' Metal Seal can help to prevent it. The liquid can also be used to coat and protect guns placed in storage (and isn't nearly as messy as gun grease). The material also has lubricating qualities so that it can be used in place of oil. Metal Seal is available at most gun shops and carries a retail tag of about $3.75 for a six-ounce container.

There are many good cleaning products on the market for those who need to tackle cleaning a pistol that's been "through the works" in the way of excessive shooting without cleaning or that's been used in a very dirty environment. Among the best of these are Outers' Crud Cutter and Nitro Solvent (they do just what their names suggest). For blasting bits of sand or other debris from hard-to-reach areas inside the Ruger frame, the Grit Getter is ideal; a few blasts from this aerosol can of compressed air will generally blow grit clear of the pistol's workings. (And, yes, a manufacturer has finally figured out a way to sell cans of air!) All three products should be available at local gun shops and carry price tags under $4.

The Ruger pistol doesn't require any special tools for maintenance, though a plastic or rubber mallet can be of use with tight new guns. Drift punches, needle-nosed pliers, and gunsmith screwdrivers (with narrow blades) are useful if detailed stripping is called for; small screwdrivers will be needed to adjust the sights on target models of the Ruger.

Nearly as important as good tools is a soft surface on the workbench so that the pistol doesn't get scratched as work is being done on it. Small containers (or an ice-cube tray) are also useful for holding small parts during major disassembly of the gun.

Of greatest importance is that a shooter know enough not to tackle more gunsmithing work than he can handle. More firearms are damaged by improper disassembly/reassembly techniques than by wear and tear; this is especially true of a quality firearm like the Ruger pistol.

FIELD-STRIPPING THE RUGER PISTOL

The various models of the Ruger pistols field-strip iden-
tically. When removing the back strap of the pistol, it's wise
to notice how it is aligned in the pistol and to give a little
study to the gun's owner's manual. This can prevent head-
aches when it comes time to reassemble the pistol.

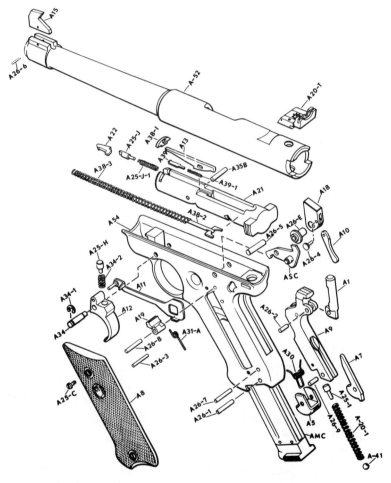

**Exploded diagram of Mark I Target Pistol. Except for the barrel and
sights, the parts are identical to those of the Standard and Bull Barrel
models. (Drawing courtesy of Sturm, Ruger and Company.)**

Like many other pistols, the Rugers are a bit tedious to field-strip the first few times out, and reassembly is even harder than the takedown until the owner learns the trick of getting the hammer down and its strut into position.

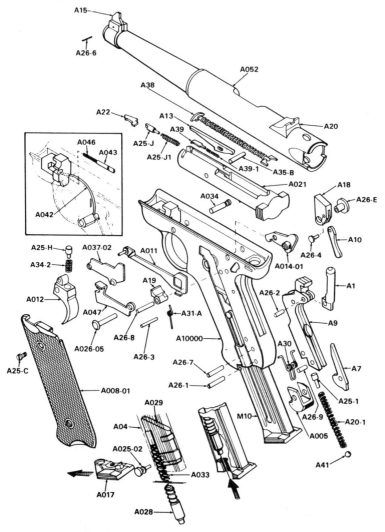

Exploded diagram of Mark II Standard Pistol. The parts are identical to those of the Mark II Target and Bull Barrel models, except for the barrel and sights. (Drawing courtesy of Sturm, Ruger and Company.)

A-52	Barrel/receiver assembly		M-10*	Magazine (Mark II series)
A052*	Barrel/receiver assembly (Mark II series)		A017*	Magazine block, bottom (Mark II series)
A-21	Bolt		A028*	Magazine-block retaining plunger (Mark II series)
A021*	Bolt (Mark II)			
A037-02*	Bolt-stop assembly (Mark II series only)		A04*	Magazine body (Mark II series)
A1	Bolt-stop pin		A029*	Magazine follower (Mark II series)
A26-2	Bolt-stop retaining pin		A025-02*	Magazine-follower button (Mark II series)
A043*	Bolt-stop plunger (Mark II series only)			
A046*	Bolt-stop plunger spring (Mark II series only)		A5	Magazine latch
			A005*	Magazine latch (Mark II series)
A047*	Bolt-stop thumb piece (Mark II series only)		A26-1	Magazine latch pin
			A30	Magazine latch spring
A11	Disconnector		A26-7	Magazine latch spring stop pin
A011*	Disconnector (Mark II series)		A033*	Magazine spring (Mark II series)
A22	Extractor			
A25-J	Extractor plunger		A-20-1	Mainspring
A25-J-1	Extractor plunger spring		A-41	Mainspring detent
			A9	Mainspring housing
A13	Firing pin		A25-1	Mainspring plunger
A35B	Firing-pin retaining pin		A20	Rear sight (Standard)
			A20-T	Rear target sight
A39	Firing-pin support		A38-3	Recoil spring
A39-1	Firing-pin support spring		A38-2	Recoil spring guide
			A38-1	Recoil spring retainer
A54	Frame			
A10000*	Frame (Mark II series)		ASC	Safety
			A014-01*	Safety (Mark II series)
A15	Front-sight blade			
BB-36	Front-sight blade (Bull Barrel T512)		A19	Sear
			A26-8	Sear pivot pin
A15-T	Front-sight blade (Target-T678)		A31-A	Sear spring
			A26-3	Sear-spring stop pin
A26-6	Front-sight pin		A12	Trigger
A-8	Grip plate		A012*	Trigger (Mark II series)
A008-01*	Grip plate (Mark II series)			
			A34	Trigger pivot
A25-C	Grip plate screw (4 needed)		A034*	Trigger pivot (Mark II series)
A18	Hammer		A34-1	Trigger-pivot lock washer (Standard/Mark I series)
A26-E	Hammer bushing			
A26-5	Hammer pivot		A042*	Trigger-pivot retainer spring (Mark II series)
A026-05*	Hammer pivot (Mark II series)			
A10	Hammer strut		A34-2	Trigger spring
A26-4	Hammer strut pin		A25-H	Trigger-spring plunger
A7	Housing latch			
A26-9	Housing latch pin			
AMC	Magazine (Standard and Mark I)			

Asterisks denote a Mark II part that is different from that of the Standard/Mark I series of pistols.

Disassembly

If parts differ between older and newer guns—or between models—the first number is that of the older or Standard pistol; the second number is that of the newer Mark I/II. Use the owner's manual or the exploded diagrams in this book to locate various parts. Here's the disassembly procedure:

1) Remove the magazine (part AMC or M-10 on the exploded diagrams or in the Sturm, Ruger & Company manuals). Cycle the pistol to be sure it's empty and then release the bolt (A21 or A021 on diagram).

2) Place the safety in its "fire" position, and pull the trigger (A12) to be sure the internal hammer is down. (Target shooters who often field-strip their guns for cleaning will want to place an empty brass cartridge in the chamber before dropping the hammer to keep from dinging up the chamber.)

3) Release the housing latch (A7) in the recess at the rear of the grip.

4) Swing the main spring housing (A9) out and pull the bolt-stop pin (A1) out and down from the receiver.

5) Remove the bolt assembly through the rear of the receiver.

6) Push the rear of the barrel/receiver assembly (A-52 or A052) forward to remove it from the frame. With some new pistols, the fit may be tight and a soft mallet will be needed to knock the receiver/barrel unit forward. Take care to use a soft mallet: a hard hammer or off-center blow can damage the pistol. (For those not having three hands, the proper procedure to follow to keep from dropping half the pistol is to hold the mallet in one hand and wrap the pinkie and ring fingers of the other hand around the pistol grip with the thumb around the rear of the grip and the middle finger in the trigger guard. The first finger can then be placed over the receiver so that the barrel receiver won't fall off and be damaged when it comes free.)

7) With M-10 magazines, the magazine can be easily disassembled for cleaning by using a small piece of wire to push up the magazine block retaining plug (A028). This releases the magazine block (A017), or floor plate, so that it can be slid forward. Take care, as the retaining lug is under spring pressure. (Note that the magazine follower button [A025-02] goes on the left side of the magazine during reassembly, and the small end of the retaining plug points down.)

The takedown latch is clearly shown on the rear of the pistol grip of this Mark II Standard. (Photo courtesy of Sturm, Ruger and Company.)

This completes the field-stripping procedures that will allow you to clean the pistol fully. Further disassembly is not recommended, though it may occasionally be necessary to remove the recoil spring, firing pin, or extractor as outlined below in order to clean the pistol after extended use.

Using a screwdriver or knife blade to release the housing latch will scratch the finish if care isn't taken; using fingernails is asking for a broken nail. The best solution to the problem is to use the inner loop of a paper clip or other tool made of rounded wire that won't skin up the metal of the gun.

Reassembly is basically a reversal of the above procedure, but there are a few tricks. First, *after* the bolt is in place, be sure the hammer (A18) is forward, not cocked back (it is released by pointing the barrel down and pulling the trigger). Second, the hammer strut (A10) must stick back and down toward the slot in the rear of the pistol grip; it must be fitted into the small depression in the forward side of the main spring housing (A9).

To reassemble:

1) Be sure the safety is in the fire position, and then place the barrel/receiver assembly (A52 or A052) on the frame and push it backward (again, the muzzle of the barrel may need to be *lightly* tapped with the mallet to drive it home or the muzzle placed down on a heavy magazine and the pistol grip pushed down against it).

2) Place the hammer back by pointing the muzzle up and pulling the trigger.

3) Slide the bolt (A21 or A021) into the rear of the barrel/receiver unit (A52), being careful that the right side of the bolt is up (the spring is on top and the extractor (A22) is to the right of the firearm when properly aligned).

4) Place the hammer (A18) forward inside the pistol frame by pointing the barrel down and pulling the trigger.

5) Place the main spring bolt-stop pin (A1) into the base of the receiver and through its hole in the barrel. The recoil spring guide may appear to block the hole, but when the

stop pin is pushed against it, the guide will go forward slightly to allow it clearance.

6) Point the barrel upward (at about 60 degrees from straight up). Make sure the hammer strut (A10) is hanging down so that it rests on the main spring depression.

7) With the strut in place, latch the main spring unit shut and lock the housing latch (A7).

8) If the hammer isn't forward, the mainspring assembly won't go together or latch shut. If the strut is in the wrong position, the bolt won't cock after the pistol is assembled. If either of these conditions exists, take out the mainspring housing and continue from step 3 above of the reassembly procedure.

As consolation to the novice, reassembly can be quite tedious the first few times you try it. The pistol owner is well advised to allow ample time for the task (i.e., don't try it just before you start shooting in competition). At the same time, most "old timers" find that, with practice, they can actually reassemble the Ruger pistol in less than a minute once they get the feel of when the hammer strut is in place. After one becomes accustomed to the gun, there is no problem in taking it apart and reassembling it.

With brand-new pistols, finicky shooters may want to use a small file to "break" some of the sharp edges on the barrel and frame when it is first field-stripped. While the edges aren't normally sharp enough to cause cuts, they can be uncomfortable if the firearm is to be detail stripped. The file should be used to *lightly* go over any sharp edges, with care taken not to cause any file marks.

Anyone concerned about having to use a mallet to disassemble/assemble his pistol can get a looser fit by taking the pistol to a gunsmith. The work might even be tackled by a do-it-yourselfer *provided* time and care were taken to do it right.

The work is done by using a fine-toothed file to carefully remove metal from the lower side of the barrel/receiver assembly where the unit touches the front and rear of the grip frame. The exact points where the metal should be removed can be seen on most "tight" guns as small, shiny scratch marks on the receiver. Care must be taken to remove only a little metal at a time until the proper fit is achieved. File work should be done perpendicular to the receiver so that file teeth move with the finishing marks on the pistol; if this is done with a fine file, no refinishing will be needed on stainless steel models and touch-up blue will cover the work on blued guns.

Ideally, the fit should be a bit tight; loose-goose guns will allow dirt to get into them and may even clank a bit. *Do not* remove any metal from the locking lug created by the upper trigger guard, from the hole in the receiver where the lug locks, or from the pistol frame.

The force needed to release the frame latch can also be decreased by carefully smoothing its nose when the mainspring assembly is removed and the latch shoved into its fully open position. The small nose only should be smoothed; care should be taken not to remove too much metal or the latch will fail to engage the detent ball and will no longer lock up the assembly.

DETAIL-STRIPPING THE RUGER PISTOL

For most Ruger pistol owners, detail-stripping the firearm will never be necessary. Such work should never be done unless absolutely needed since there is always the chance of damaging the pistol, losing a part, or just making the pistol "wear fit" parts together again after they've been shifted about. It's also easy to damage a firearm during detail-stripping if a shooter doesn't know what he's doing. Gunsmiths pick up a lot of work because gun owners try to disassemble firearms when there's no need to do so. The old saying, "If it ain't broke, don't fix it," certainly applies here.

It is also essential to use quality tools when working on a firearm. A make-do drift punch can be constructed from a nail and common mallets, and will work, but it's *very* important to use gunsmithing screwdrivers when removing the grips or adjusting target sights (these are the only places screws are used on the Ruger pistols) in order not to damage the slots. Such screwdrivers and other tools are available in most gun stores or can be ordered from B-Square Company.

For those who wish to replace the magazine release, trigger, or other part with an aftermarket product, it's also wise to only do enough disassembly work to get to the part in question so that it can be replaced.

Most of the parts in the Standard/Mark I series are the same as those of the Mark II series. Where there is a difference, the Standard/Mark I numbers are given first in parentheses, and the second part number is that used for the Mark II series. In general, these numbers are the same, with an "0" inserted after the "A" for each change made from the original design (those wanting to keep track of changes might use this to provide a clue when looking at old Ruger manuals and company literature).

Before detail-stripping, the gun should be field-stripped following the seven steps outlined above. That done, the steps below can be carried out. Steps should be skipped, when possible, if certain parts don't need to be reached for repair, adjustment, or replacement. Wearing protective glasses during this or other gunsmith-type work is a wise precaution.

8) The recoil spring (A38-3) and its guide (A38-2) can be removed by simply pushing the guide forward and lifting the unit up out of the top of the bolt (A-21). The recoil spring retainer (A38-1) is riveted in place by a split in the end of the guide rod, so the spring should not be removed from the guide unless absolutely necessary.

9) The firing pin (A13) can be removed by pushing out the retaining pin (A35B) with a drift punch. The bolt should be inspected to be sure the pin isn't "staked" on one side. Once the pin is clear, the firing pin can be lifted out of its slot on the top of the bolt. (Staking is done with a small punch that is used to push bits of metal over a pin to keep it in place. This is generally done on just one side so that the pin can be removed by pushing from the staked side.)

10) The firing pin support (A39) and its rebound spring (A39-1) can be removed from the top of the bolt after the firing pin is taken out.

11) The extractor (A22) and its plunger (A25-J) and plunger spring (A25-J-1) can be released by depressing the extractor spring plunger with a small tool and wiggling the extractor out of its place. This done, the plunger can be released and it and its spring removed. (Care should be taken, as the spring is under a lot of tension.)

12) The grip panels (A-8 or A008-01) can be removed by unscrewing the two screws (A25-C) holding each of them in place. Be sure to use a gunsmithing screwdriver to prevent damage to the heads of the screws. Once the panels are removed, access will be given to the pins holding the hammer, magazine release, and so on. (Gunsmithing screwdrivers can generally be found at gun shops or ordered from Brownells, Inc. Refer to Appendix A.)

13) The largest pin at the top of the frame that was covered by the grip panels is the hammer pivot (A26-5 or A026-05), which holds the hammer (A18), hammer strut (A10), hammer bushing (A26-E), and hammer strut pin (A26-4). If this pin is drifted out to the left of the frame, the parts can be lifted up out of the frame; on the Mark II pistols, the bolt-stop thumb piece (A047) will be released as well when this pin is removed. The hammer and its parts are then separated from the disconnector (A11 or A011)—which is connected to the trigger—by pushing out the hammer bushing. Pushing out the hammer strut pin will separate it from the hammer. Take care to note the placement of parts before disassembling them.

14) The safety (ASC or A014-01) can be lifted out by moving it inward and out the top of the frame. No attempt should be made to further disassemble the safety.

15) The sear (A19) and its spring (A31-A) can be freed by pushing out the pivot pin (A26-8) below the hammer pin. The small sear-spring stop pin (A26-3) below the sear pin is used to hold the tail end of the sear spring in place. Take note of the way the spring and sear are mounted in the

pistol before removing them.

16) The lower pin at the rear of the pistol grip is the magazine latch pin (A26-1). It can be drifted out to release the magazine latch (A5 or A005) and its spring (A30). The pin (A26-7) above the catch holds the tail of the spring in place. Again, note the positioning of the parts before removing them.

17) The trigger pivot (A34) is held in place by a C-clip lock washer (A34-1) on the Standard and Mark I pistols and by a piano-wire clip (A042) on the Mark II series. Removing the C-clip or simply pushing the piano-wire loop back toward the rear of the receiver will free the trigger pin, which can be taken out through the side of the receiver. This will allow removal of the trigger (A12 or A012), disconnector (A11 or A011), trigger spring (A34-2), and trigger spring plunger (A25-H).

18) On Mark II models, the bolt-stop plunger (A043) and its spring (A046) will be released when the bolt-stop assembly (A037-02) is freed by removing the trigger pivot pin; care must be taken, since the plunger spring is under pressure. No attempt should be made to disassemble the disconnector or bolt-stop assembly since the small parts on them are riveted in place. On Mark II pistols, the overtravel adjustment screw is located on the upper front side of the trigger; adjustment of this shouldn't be too fine, as a little dirt could put a too closely regulated trigger out of commission. If the set screw is readjusted, apply lacquer (nail polish) so that it won't jiggle loose.

19) The rear sight (A20 or A20-T depending on the type of sight) can be removed by drifting it out of the upper receiver; many target sights have a set screw that must first be loosened. The front sight (A15) can be removed by drifting out the pin (A26-6) holding it in place. (Note: Rear and front sights vary from one Ruger pistol version to another, and replacement front sights may need to have the pinhole drilled in them before they can be installed.)

20) The bolt-stop pin (A1) is usually staked in place and can be removed from the mainspring housing only through

many blows with a drift punch and hammer. Therefore, if at all possible, the pin (A26-2) should not be removed (should it be removed, the process may damage the mainspring housing so that it will then need to be replaced). This work is best left to a gunsmith.

21) The housing latch (A7) is also staked to the mainspring (A-20-1). The plunger (A25-1) and its detent ball (A-41) can be removed by drifting the latch pivot pin. But, as with the bolt-stop pin, this is generally best left undone, since removal may damage the housing. Furthermore, the mainspring is under tension, thereby making replacement difficult. (Should the housing latch/mainspring be disassembled, one gunsmithing trick in getting it back together is to drill a small hole—about 0.05 inches in diameter—through the spring well about opposite the cup cut in the heel of the assembly for the housing latch. This will allow the insertion of a small wire nail through the housing. Once in place, the spring can be wound onto the nail with a pair of needle-nose pliers. With the nail holding the spring, the detent ball can then be placed in the spring well and the housing latch and its pin put over it without having to overcome the spring pressure. Once everything is secure, the nail is withdrawn and the spring activates the ball and latch.)

22) The ejector (not shown, A16) is riveted to a bar on the lower side of the receiver. The rivet can be removed by grinding off the exposed end. Replacing it calls for an anvil to be made which can be fitted into the receiver to hold the ejector and new rivet (not shown, A25-A) in place. The exposed end is then peened into place to secure the ejector. This is also a job for a gunsmith, and no attempt should be made to remove it unless it's broken.

23) A target sight (A20-T) can be disassembled by drifting out the small pin (MR-56) at its front and unscrewing the elevation screw. Take care not to lose the small elevation spring under the assembly. Note that the small set screw must be loosened before the sight base can be drifted out.

****

Reassembly is basically a reversal of the above procedure.

EMERGENCY REPAIR KITS

All mechanical things eventually wear out with heavy use, but the Ruger pistols are noted for not breaking or wearing out. Like other Ruger firearms, the pistols are justly described as "gunsmith's nightmares" since they don't give these workers much business. With this in mind, emergency repair kits aren't really called for unless you're careless when cleaning the pistol, dissassemble it and lose some parts, or monkey with the firearm and damage it.

The *only* part that it's wise to have spares of is the magazine. In addition to making it possible to carry more ammunition for the pistol in a ready-to-go state, damaging a magazine (which is easy to do with metal box magazines) won't put the gun out of commission at a critical moment.

For those who really worry about such things, an emergency kit with a few essential parts that are prone to more wear than others in most firearms might be an investment just to ease one's mind. Parts to consider purchasing are the extractor, extractor plunger and its spring, ejector and its rivet, firing pin, and recoil spring. Also worth considering buying are some of the smaller parts that might be lost or broken, such as grip screws, firing-pin rebound spring support, bolt hold-open plunger and its spring, and various pins.

If you opt for purchasing parts, first try Ruger's Product Service Department at Southport, CT 06490, which sells parts for a nominal price; prices are usually listed in owner's manuals. (These should come with the firearm. If you don't have a manual with your gun, contact Ruger for a free one.) Ruger pistols that need to be repaired can also be shipped to this address.

When parts are ordered from Sturm, Ruger & Company, the pistol's model and serial number should be included, as there are slight variations in parts from one model to another, as well as within each model series. The owner of the firearm should also take care in replacing parts, as it's easy to ruin the gun's reliability if parts aren't properly assembled and/or fitted.

MODIFICATIONS TO THE RUGER PISTOLS

Modifying any firearm should be approached with extreme caution; poor modifications will make a firearm unreliable and even the simplest changes will usually void any warranty that may have come with the firearm. Shooters shouldn't tinker with a firearm unless a change really needs to be made.

Probably the simplest modification to a Ruger .22 pistol is to purchase a "bolt-on" accessory. Nearly all these can be placed on the firearm without the need of a gunsmith.

One exception to this is trigger work or the replacement of the trigger. If, for some reason, such work is needed, lightening the pull or other work is best left to a gunsmith. (The pull of the Ruger can be lightened and smoothed; the Clark trigger, as well as Ruger's target trigger and other replacements, are also available to gunsmiths and may be of use to some shooters. These accessories are discussed in Chapter 4.)

In general, the fewer changes made to a Ruger .22 pistol, the less apt something is to go wrong with it. Therefore, give it a lot of thought before having one of these firearms modified.

TROUBLESHOOTING

The Ruger pistols are noted for their reliability. But firearms, being mechanical things, do occasionally fail. As noted elsewhere, one of the main causes of failure is damage caused when a firearm is improperly disassembled/reassembled or modified by someone who doesn't know what he's doing. Other failures are often caused by extensive fouling (which is especially possible with extended shooting of cheap ammunition) or by using poor ammunition.

Although Ruger pistols function with great reliability right from the box (they are test-fired at the factory to be sure they work and are accurate), like other firearms, they will generally function at peak reliability after being broken in with a few hundred rounds. This is so because use causes rough edges to be rounded off, and bearing surfaces tend to polish themselves as they slide over each other. This occurs after firing the pistol for a short time, after which parts will be "custom fit" to each other. (For those wishing to save a bit of cash, much the same type of "fitting" can be done by hand-cycling the pistol a number of times, though not all parts are affected nor does this work nearly as well as does actually shooting the firearm.)

Avoid dry-firing the Ruger, as doing so can weaken or even break the firing pin over extended periods. It can also cause the chamber to become peened where the firing pin hits it. If the gun must be dry-fired, place an empty brass case in it to absorb some of the energy of the firing pin.

Keeping a pistol clean will improve functioning and prevent the excessive wear that can occur if grit or sand gets into its action. A clean Ruger lasts longer and is less apt to fail than an identical—but dirty—gun.

When using the pistol outside, avoid firing a round with a barrel obstruction. A misfire that lodges a bullet in the barrel, a bug looking for a home, or a plug of snow or dirt can all cause the barrel to rupture ("goose egg") when the gun is fired. Always be sure the bore is clear.

If a pistol fails to fire, here are some quick steps that can be carried out to be sure some simple thing hasn't caused the failure:

1) The magazine should be tapped to be sure it's seated.

2) The action should be pulled back and the chamber locked open while a visual inspection is made to be sure a case was ejected and a shell isn't jammed in the chamber.

3) If the chamber is clear, the bolt should be released to chamber a new round. Care should be taken *not* to "ride"

the bolt forward; rather, the recoil spring should slam the bolt home with full force. (To check whether a round is chambered, the shooter should pull back slightly on the bolt and peek into the chamber. Once satisfied, he should push the bolt fully forward.)

4) The safety should be checked to be sure it's in the "fire" position.

5) The shooter should try to shoot the pistol again.

6) If the Ruger fails to fire, the shooter should go through the above steps one more time.

7) If the pistol still fails to function, the magazine should be removed and the gun cycled to be sure it's empty. That done, the bolt should be locked open and the inside of the ejection port area inspected for an obstruction or broken part.

8) If a fault isn't found, the shooter should change magazines, cycle the action, and try to fire again.

Even if these steps are followed and the pistol is clean and well maintained, it may still fail on rare occasions. The best bet is to take the pistol to a gunsmith for repair.

If, however, a shooter isn't able to do so because he's in the middle of nowhere or is using the pistol for self-defense or as a survival gun, knowing how to get the pistol to function again may be essential and—in extreme situations—might even mean the difference between life and death. In such a case, the shooter should be familiar with the following procedures so that he will know how to get his firearm into firing condition without the aid of a skilled gunsmith.

The reader should be forewarned: *Many of the following procedures are dangerous.* No one should carry out any of these steps unless it is *absolutely necessary,* as he may be risking life and limb to carry them out. Generally, most cases in which a firearm fails will not warrant taking such a risk; the best bet is to take the firearm to a gunsmith.

****

Ruger .22 Pistol Troubleshooting Procedures

Problem	Check	Procedure
Bolt does not hold open after last round (Mark II).	Fouled/broken bolt latch	Clean/replace.
Bolt won't close.	Fouling in bolt face	Clean and lubricate.
	Recoil spring is not moving freely.	Remove, clean, and lubricate.
	Bolt is not moving freely.	Remove, clean, and lubricate.
	Bent spring guide	Check alignment; replace or straighten.
	Damaged recoil spring	Replace.
	Dirty recoil spring	Remove and clean.
Bolt won't open.	Dirty or burred bolt	Clean or replace.
Firearm won't cock; safety doesn't work properly.	Worn, broken, or missing parts	Check parts; replace.
Firearm continues to fire after release of trigger.	Dirt in trigger/sear	Clean mechanism.
	Broken sear/trigger	Replace.
	Weak sear/trigger spring	Replace.

Ruger .22 Pistol Troubleshooting Procedures (cont.)

Problem	Check	Procedure
Firearm continues to fire after release of trigger (cont.).	Broken disconnector	Replace.
Firearm won't fire.	Safety in "Safe" position	Place in "fire" position.
	Firing pin is broken.	Replace.
	Too much oil or dirt in firing-pin recess	Wipe/clean.
	Poor ammo	Remove/discard.
	Mainspring is dirty or broken.	Clean or replace.
Round won't chamber.	Dirty or corroded ammo	Clean or replace ammo.
	Damaged ammo	Replace.
	Fouling in chamber	Clean with chamber brush.
Rounds won't eject.	Broken ejector	Replace.
Rounds won't extract.	Dirty/corroded ammo	Remove (may have to be carefully pushed out with cleaning rod). Caution: *This procedure can be very dangerous.*

Ruger .22 Pistol Troubleshooting Procedures (cont.)

Problem	Check	Procedure
Rounds won't extract (cont.).	Broken extractor or bad extractor spring	Replace.
	Fouling in chamber or extractor lip	Clean chamber and lip.
	Dirty/faulty recoil spring	Clean/replace.
	Dirt in extractor groove in barrel	Clean.
Rounds won't feed.	Dirty or corroded ammo	Clean ammo.
	Low-powered ammo or poorly shaped nose on bullets in cartridges	Use different ammo.
	Defective magazine	Replace magazine.
	Dirt in magazine	Clean magazine.
	Magazine not seated	Reseat/replace magazine.
	Broken magazine catch	Repair/replace.
Safety binds.	Dirt/lack of lubrication	Lubricate; if it still binds, clean with soft brush.

Ruger .22 Pistol Troubleshooting Procedures (cont.)

Problem	Check	Procedure
Short recoil (New rounds fail to chamber.)	Poor ammunition	Replace.

PURCHASING A USED RUGER

With Sturm, Ruger & Company going for their two-millionth .22 semiauto pistol, you'd think the gun shops would be full of used Rugers for sale. In fact, the Ruger isn't commonly sold used as often as many pistols and revolvers of which there have been many fewer made. That owners of the Ruger .22 are slow to part with it speaks well of the Ruger's long-lasting quality.

But Ruger pistols do, on occasion, show up on the used gun market for one reason or another and can be good buys for those who don't have a lot of cash—provided the gun hasn't been damaged.

And how does a would-be buyer tell whether the gun was owned by a little old lady who never fired it or by a madman who used it for a hammer on the weekends?

For starters, the customer should ask around and find a reputable gun dealer. (It's been my experience that a huge percentage of gun dealers are very aboveboard and are good businessmen. There are, though, a very few who are just one step ahead of the federal agents and sell firearms that barely work or are of dubious backgrounds. Needless to say, it's better not to ever get mixed up with such folks.)

Once a store with a good reputation is found, the buyer should carefully inspect the Ruger pistol before making any offer to buy it (and if the dealer isn't willing to let a customer give the gun a good look, the would-be buyer should look elsewhere).

When inspecting a gun, look at the wear and tear on the outside of the pistol. Is the bluing worn? Worn bluing may result just from holster wear; if so, this isn't too serious, though it can lower the pistol's price. Touch-up blue can cure the problem and make the pistol a good buy if it is otherwise in good shape.

How about deep nicks that suggest the gun had some rough treatment? If these are present, you would do well to think hard before buying the gun. Be sure to inspect it thoroughly.

Do you see rust, deep pits where rust has been (gun dealers and previous owners can know about touch-up blue, too), or broken parts? If so, the buyer is advised to look at another gun, since the pistol hasn't been well cared for and probably has internal damage as well.

Shaking the gun shouldn't reveal any loud rattles; the sights should be steady and not readily moved when firmly touched. The pistol should be carefully inspected for anything that appears out of the ordinary.

Ideally, a potential buyer will next inspect the bore if the pistol has passed the initial external inspection. Unfortunately, most buyers don't have a bore light handy, and it isn't fair to expect the gun dealer to have one either (though, if the customer is serious about buying, he could always ask). A make-do situation can be carried out if some bright light (say, near a window) is available. In such a case, locking the bolt open (with the safety on the Mark I or with the bolt hold-open lever with the Mark II), pointing the ejection port toward the light source, and peering down the muzzle may reveal what kind of shape the bore is in.

What should the customer be looking for? First, the bore should be carefully examined for rust, rust pits, scratches, or rough spots. While a bulged or bent barrel isn't too common, a ring or bright area may show where such damage has occurred. If the pistol is to be used for anything other than plinking, any of these conditions is a reason to reject purchasing the gun.

Next, the muzzle of the pistol should be checked. There shouldn't be any nicks or scratches which go in the crown (inside edge) of the muzzle as this will damage the pistol's accuracy. It is also wise to check the crown for rust if this hasn't already been done. The muzzle should also be checked for damage to the rifling that might have occurred if the pistol has been cleaned from that end rather than from the chamber end. (Even though a gunsmith can cut off a portion of the muzzle and recrown it, doing so can be an expensive proposition since the front sight will have to be moved back. Having such work done isn't a good way to save money unless a really expensive custom gun is being examined—and chances of that are slim.)

With the bolt still locked back, the chamber and bolt face are next examined. These areas also need to be checked for rust, pits, or deep scratches. Deep pitting or scratches in the chamber can cause extraction problems, a good reason to reject the pistol. It's hard to see much without a bore light, but erosion in the chamber may also show up; this can be caused by firing large numbers of .22 Shorts in the .22 LR chamber, another good reason to reject the gun. If a bore light isn't available, erosion may still show up in the form of crud built up at the front of the chamber, which would prevent a .22 LR—but not a Short—cartridge from being chambered.

Next, the top face of the chamber opposite the firing pin should be checked for peening that can take place with extended dry-firing. This peening can be repaired by a gunsmith but, again, doing so costs some extra money, and you'd do better to pass on such a pistol.

Because dry-firing can damage the firing pin or chamber face, most gun dealers won't be keen on having a would-be buyer cycle and snap off the empty gun. The solution to this is for the buyer to have some spent cases that can be shown to the dealer, along with the test proposal. This will usually meet with approval.

After the bolt is closed over the empty cartridge, a number of things can be discovered about the gun. First, is the trigger pull good or is it creepy? Is it extremely light?

(This may show that an amateur has "reworked" it and left it in a damaged condition, especially if the pistol isn't a target gun.)

After dry-firing, the cartridge should be examined to be sure the firing pin has struck it with enough force to leave a second, deep mark on the rim of the shell. Also, the new indentation will tell whether the firing pin is worn or damaged. A shallow indentation means the firing pin is damaged or the mainspring is weak; either one means extra gun work and maybe even a lot of extra expense.

How well did the shell extract when the gun was hand-cycled open after dry-firing? The answer to this may reveal whether the extractor is malfunctioning or whether the chamber is damaged.

If possible, the shooter should place an empty cartridge in the chamber and then tightly pull the trigger back, keeping it back as the bolt is closed. Once the bolt is closed, the trigger should be released and pulled again. If the hammer followed the bolt forward so that the hammer doesn't drop (because it is already forward) when the trigger is pulled the second time, the sear or disconnector is damaged and the firearm is potentially dangerous since it might slam-fire or even go into an automatic mode.

Finally, if the pistol has passed all these hurdles, it is desirable to fire it before purchasing it to be absolutely certain the pistol will work right. This isn't generally possible except in some very large gun shops, but most reputable gun dealers will make good on a deal if the buyer takes the gun home and discovers it doesn't work. The key here is to take the gun out to a range *immediately* after purchase to check it out for functioning. Taking a gun back a few hours after purchase because it doesn't work is going to suggest the buyer needs restitution; taking it back days or weeks after purchase suggests that the buyer has screwed up the gun on his own.

Buying a used Ruger can save the buyer some cash *if* he takes the time and care to really check out the pistol before purchasing it.

Chapter 4

Accessories

As with other popular firearms, there are many gadgets and accessories made for Ruger pistols. Accessories can help adapt a firearm to an individual's needs, but they can also make a Ruger pistol awkward or heavy if care isn't taken to choose accessories wisely.

All that's really needed for most shooters is quality ammunition, a few spare magazines, and a good holster; it is usually a good idea for most shooters to refrain from buying any other accessories for the Ruger pistols. A few shooters may also benefit from a special grip or scope mount. However, owners of this pistol should keep in mind that any additional accessory may not really be needed and is often money poorly spent.

That said, here's a look at some of the gear and gadgets available to Ruger pistol owners:

BARRELS

There's nothing wrong with the Ruger pistol's barrel. Those wanting lightweight barrels can go with the Ruger 4 3/4-inch Standard model; obtaining a long barrel for maximum velocity with most .22 LR ammunition is simply a matter of purchasing a Mark II with a 10-inch Bull Barrel (MK-10 or KMK-10). For the ultimate in accuracy, there's the MK-678-G.

The catch comes for those wanting to exchange barrel/receiver assemblies so that one frame assembly can serve double or triple duty with different barrels. Though physically practical, the barrel/receivers aren't that easy to purchase since they bear the serial number for the pistol. As such, they are registered as firearms, and a Federal Firearms License (FFL) and paperwork are required before these items can be legally purchased. In fact, Sturm, Ruger & Company doesn't even offer the barrel/receivers for sale unless they're part of a whole pistol.

For those who can locate one of the AMT Lightning barrel/receivers to add to that which came with their Ruger, such a setup certainly adds a bit of flexibility to the system. One might be able to switch the barrel/receivers to have a knock-about gun with a nice trigger pull for camping trips or a target gun for competition events. Unfortunately, this isn't very easy to do at the time of this writing. (It would be nice if Sturm, Ruger & Company started offering "combos" of a pistol with two different barrel styles. Doing so would create a lot of extra work in the shipping room and would disrupt the assembly line, making chances these combos would be sold rather remote.)

For maximum barrel weight reduction, it's also possible to mount a lightweight barrel designed for silencers from Cobray on a Ruger receiver (see below). The catch, though, is that getting barrels off the receiver of Ruger pistols is not a simple task; generally, the old barrel has to be cut off just ahead of the receiver and then reamed out until its threads collapse so that it can be removed. In addition to the barrel being destroyed, damage can result to the receiver if the work isn't done skillfully. Replacing the barrel is best done by a qualified gunsmith.

When a Ruger has a silencer barrel placed on it, without a legal silencer mounted, care needs to be taken not to damage the lightweight barrel. It is also wise to place a small nut on the threads if the user plans to ever use the pistol with a real (or fake) silencer, muzzle brakes, flash hiders, or the like.

Those wanting a Douglas target barrel or a cut-down .22 target-rifle barrel blank mounted on a Ruger will need to go through much the same procedure. Such work is definitely a job for a skilled gunsmith since the Douglas blank must be chambered and both need to be threaded, have a feed ramp cut into them, flats cut, the extractor cut made, and—finally—the barrel mounted to the receiver.

If a local gunsmith doesn't want to tackle this work, the best bet is to contact Tom Volquartsen for such work; his company also carries a number of customized Ruger pistols with target barrels, which makes it possible to simply buy the target pistol you need rather than having one modified.

All in all, a shooter's money is probably better spent simply buying a second Ruger pistol to do the new task that the first gun can't quite cut. Given the low price tags the pistols carry (compared to the cost and troubles of getting a new barrel/receiver or having a barrel replaced), buying another pistol is usually the quickest and easiest route to take.

RIFLE STOCKS AND WRIST BRACES

As mentioned earlier, most experienced pistol shooters using a two-handed hold can score shots as accurate as when they use a pistol having a rifle-style stock. Novice shooters do, however, initially experience better shooting with shoulder stocks.

A stock actually attached to a pistol is illegal in the United States without a special permit. However, several companies have made stocks that are only held in place on the pistol when it is fired. These are perfectly legal as things now stand and will probably remain so since it is generally recognized that such devices do little to make a handgun more dangerous or accurate. They certainly make it harder to conceal (in fact, one has to wonder why those who passed laws didn't encourage shooters to put stocks on pistols in order to make them less concealable).

Best known of these held-in-place stocks is the Assistant, which is made by Assault Accessories (see Appendix A). The device is a welded wire stock that fits around each side of the rear of the frame so that it butts up against the pistol grips and the rear of the frame under the receiver. It is held in place by the shooter's thumb. The two contoured steel wires that rest against the pistol are covered with neoprene plastic to keep them from scratching the pistol; they also help to hold the stock in place due to the friction they create on the frame.

The Assistant is well made and lightweight; while skilled shooters can get along without it, it may be put to good use by others. The cost is approximately $47.

Another variation on this idea is the Steady Grip, available from J&G Sales for about $9; the unit replaces one of the Ruger grip panels and has a wire support that extends from its lower edge to wrap around the wrist. This makes a rigid support from the forearm to the pistol and does aid in one-handed shooting (though a two-handed grip will create much the same effect). The down side of this product is that drawing the pistol becomes a longer process because the wrist has to be fitted into the Steady Grip. And carrying it in a holster is a dubious endeavor at best, as it catches on anything that comes within reach of its hooked end. In short, this device might be of use to handicapped shooters or target shooters using a one-handed grip. Most others will probably find it next to useless.

ENGINE TURNING

Engine turning, or jeweling, is created by using a spinning bit with abrasive on its end to create swirl patterns on a piece of steel. These patterns are generally made in groups so that the result is a number of tiny circles coating the side of a metal part.

In addition to being decorative, these swirls help smooth the action of parts as well. While it would seem that the greater surface area created by these patterns would increase the friction on them, what actually happens is that the tiny grooves hold more oil. The part then actually glides on the oil and moves more smoothly than if the surface were perfectly polished and smooth.

Engine turning is generally best left to a gunsmith, but some do-it-yourselfers with access to a drill press may wish to try their hand at it. If so, skill should be attained practicing on scrap steel, as one mistake on a pistol part can ruin its appearance.

For do-it-yourself jeweling "on the cheap," a new pencil can be cut in two and mounted in a drill-press chuck so that the rubber eraser is pointed down. A small disc of abrasive cloth of 100-grit or finer is cut and glued to the eraser. Another possibility is to use a pen with an ink eraser on its top; the eraser is cut flat as the work progresses, and its edges start to wear. (Of course, more professional work is done with a brush and grit compound, but the pencils will give good results.)

The piece to be jeweled should be clamped in the drill press's table and the press set for a high speed. The spinning disc grit is then brought down to touch the metal for just an instant. This will create one swirl pattern.

The work is next shifted slightly to one side so that the next swirl pattern can be created on bare metal. Patterns are generally kept in a straight line, with the swirls just touching at their edges, though overlapping and other patterns are often seen. The main thing is to keep the pattern consistent and symmetrical.

Jeweling is most often seen on the steel replacement triggers and original bolts of Ruger .22s, though it might also be done on other larger parts inside the gun. This work gets tricky on curved parts like the bolt; B-Square sells a special jig for jeweling bolts. For those interested in doing such work, this might prove to be a good investment, even if used only one time. The cost for the B-Square fixture is about $32; brushes cost approximately $1 each, and grit compound is about $3 per container.

EYE AND EAR PROTECTION

A .22 LR, fired from a pistol, makes enough racket to cause measurable loss of hearing with time; indoors, it may cause damage very quickly. Earmuffs designed to give maximum ear protection are most ideal for shooting, but—with the lowly .22—a shooter can get by with a pair of expanding, disposable plastic plugs that cost just a few pennies each and are easy to carry and not obtrusive to wear. (Those who do a lot of shooting may also want to invest in an over-the-counter product to clean out ear wax, since wax in the ear tends to be compressed with the extensive use of ear plugs. Cleaning every couple of months generally does the trick for those who shoot a lot.)

Shooters who practice indoors will find an added benefit to ear protection, since it also helps prevent flinching while shooting. While it may seem odd to some that a flinch would develop when firing a low-recoil firearm like the Ruger pistol, the noise is often what causes a flinch to develop with handguns, rather than the pistol's recoil. Hearing protection will prevent this bad habit from ever getting started.

The chances of having a Ruger pistol do anything dangerous enough to hurt a shooter's eye is pretty slim, even with a barrel obstruction. But there is always the possibility of an accident, a ruptured case, or even a stray shot from one of those dangerous folks who shoot before they look.

Consequently, owning a pair of the new polycarbonate sunglasses makes a lot of sense. Offering a terrific amount of eye protection, they are capable of actually stopping shotgun pellets and even some pistol bullets. Among the best are Brigade Quartermasters' Gargoyles and Jones Optical's wide array of stylish polycarbonate sunglasses, skiing goggles, and "combat" goggles. The price tags for these glasses are only a bit higher than for quality "designer" sunglasses, but most shooters will admit their eyesight is worth the added cost.

Several companies are also offering less stylish, but also less expensive, shooting glasses made of polycarbonate. Check the box to be sure the glasses are really made of polycarbonate rather than the more common—and considerably less strong—plastics used for sunglasses. These glasses offer a lot of protection for very little money, but they aren't quite as scratch-resistant or long-lasting, so be prepared to replace them from time to time.

FLASHLIGHT MOUNTS

The past few years have seen the mounting of flashlights on a variety of weapons, ranging from shotguns and rifles to small handguns. Such a setup can be a plus if the weapon is used for self-defense at night and a flashlight is needed. Besides freeing the hand that would normally be needed to carry the flashlight, the beam can be used as an aiming device. If a shot should be needed, the holder of the firearm/flashlight can tell about where the bullet will be impacting.

The drawback of a flashlight is that it makes a dandy target in the dark. If someone dangerous is out there, the flashlight will show him where his enemy is, and the light reflected back on the flashlight holder may even reveal the outlines of his body. A little sense needs to be exercised with such flashlights, and the pros and cons must be weighed before strapping a flashlight onto a Ruger pistol.

Choate Machine and Tool offers a steel flashlight mount designed to clamp a mini-flashlight (using AA batteries) to the barrel of a Ruger 10/22. This can be adapted to Ruger Standard guns with tapered barrels, *but* it requires a bit of adjusting with tape or shims, and it isn't perfect. The unit consists of two steel plates connected by bolts, with two channels running between the plate faces. The plates are screwed together, with one channel clamping onto the firearm's barrel and the other to the flashlight. The cost of the Choate unit is about $16.

Another route to achieve the same end would be to mount a flashlight on a scope base (see below). If a flashlight can be located which has a one-inch diameter, scope rings can be used to hold it in place. If you can't find such a size, then a smaller diameter should be secured; the shims or a tape wrap should be used to increase the diameter of the flashlight so that the rings will work with it.

For those who own a Ruger pistol with a 7/8-inch-diameter barrel (or an area of the barrel that approximates this width), there is a flashlight mount assembly available. It is commercially available from L.L. Baston as a complete kit and costs about $35.95. (The kit includes a small Mini-Lite mounting clamp and a "tapeswitch," which can be placed on the pistol grip so that the light can be quickly switched on and off. The shooter should take care to practice so that switch and trigger aren't confused at a critical moment.) L.L. Baston Company also sells the mount without switch or flashlight for about $10.

FLASH HIDERS AND MUZZLE BRAKES

Flash hiders on a .22 pistol aren't normally called for, though they might be needed for those planning to use the Ruger pistol for self-defense (especially since the majority of civilian shoot-outs seem to occur at night these days). Muzzle brakes (or compensators) are of use to rapid-fire target shooters or on the rare selective-fire conversions of the pistol; these devices port some of the gas produced by the cartridge upon ignition out the top near the muzzle

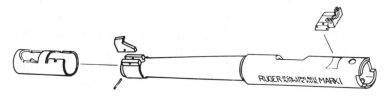

The Ruger muzzle brake was simple and easy to install. Unfortunately, it is no longer available. (Drawing courtesy of Sturm, Ruger and Company.)

(and sometimes toward the side) to counter recoil forces with a jet of hot gas.

Flash hiders and muzzle brakes can also serve a second purpose for those who use the gun outdoors: they help keep dirt out of the barrel and keep the pistol's muzzle from getting dinged up (which would ruin the gun's accuracy).

The catch to all this is that no one is currently selling flash hiders or muzzle brakes for the Ruger pistols.

For those who need a flash hider, Ram-Line offers an aluminum flash hider for the 10/22 that *might* be adaptable to a Standard pistol's tapered barrel *if* a little metal-removal work is done on the hider with a file. The cost of Ram-Line's hider is about $15.

With bull barrel guns, it's possible to cut a length of aluminum tubing that will fit over the barrel. If it is extended out over the front of the barrel, it will then offer some protection to the pistol muzzle. While flash-hider-style slots can be cut into it, they will do little to actually lessen flash; large cuts in the top, though, will help divert enough gas to actually compensate recoil forces somewhat. Placing an end cap on the tube allows the unit to work more efficiently, but it requires a lot of extra work. If it decreases the report to any extent, you might run into problems if it acts like an unauthorized silencer.

To mount a homemade tube-style muzzle brake on a bull barrel, remove the pistol's front sights and take careful measurements so that a slot can be cut into the top of the tube to allow the sights to be mounted back on the barrel. The front sight can be used to secure the tube to the barrel. (If errors are made in measurements, it is possible to use epoxy cement to more or less permanently mount the unit to the barrel.)

Perhaps a more practical alternative to the procedures outlined above is to purchase a ready-made compensator. Occasionally, an old Sturm, Ruger compensator can be located, but these have nearly all been relegated to collectors' shelves. (It is hoped that as the Ruger pistols continue to be popular, some enterprising aftermarket manufacturer will field a copy of this device.)

Probably the best route for someone really feeling a need for a flash hider or muzzle brake is to have his pistol reworked to Tom Volquartsen's Predator or a similar configuration. While such work is not cheap, the results are excellent. Until a company comes out with a readily available flash hider or compensator, this is the only option available outside of do-it-yourself work.

HOLSTERS

Without a doubt, the best deal in holsters (and holster belts) is provided by Uncle Mike's nylon holsters. These are available in black, brown, or camouflage finishes and come in a variety of sizes to accommodate various barrel lengths. Currently, Uncle Mike's offers a standard holster with a nylon snap "tie down" to keep the gun secure in the holster. Also available is a deeper holster with a detachable flap, which is ideal for carrying the pistol in rough areas or during inclement weather.

For anyone who has scoped his Ruger pistol, it's also possible to purchase from Uncle Mike's a large, vertical shoulder holster, designed for a scope-mounted pistol. The Size 3 fits pistols with a scope and 5- to 6 1/2-inch barrel; Size 4 fits 7- to 8 1/2-inch barrels, and Size 13 will work with 10-inch-barrel versions of the Ruger pistol. The holsters are available in black or camouflaged finishes.

Unlike leather, Uncle Mike's nylon holsters don't contain acids that can cause blued pistols to rust in short order. Pistols that have spent months in one of these nylon holsters don't exhibit any rust (the same can't often be said if a gun is left in a leather holster). Ballistic nylon wears as well or better than leather and is also moisture-resistant.

Uncle Mike's holsters are available at most gun stores. Prices range from about $10 to $15 for standard holsters and $30 for the vertical shoulder holster.

GRIPS

Volquartsen Custom Pistols offers a line of excellent

target grips made of wood as well as fiberglass for those who are really serious about shooting a Ruger pistol. First choice among the Volquartsen offerings are fiberglass Volthane grips, which have a full-target thumb rest, heel rest, and finger grooves. Full-target-style wooden grips of zebra wood, walnut panel-style grips (with or without thumb rests), and custom-made wooden grips made by Bowlers of England to the specifications delineated by a drawing made around the customer's hand are also available from Volquartsen. One real plus of the Volquartsen grips is that they don't have to be removed in order for the shooter to reach the back strap of the pistol during field-stripping.

The price for the Volquartsen fiberglass Volthane grips is about $40, including postage, an excellent buy for those needing target-style grips.

Brownells carries Pachmayr signature grips for the Ruger Standard/Mark I and Mark II pistols. These grips are made of neoprene rubber and have checkering cut into them, giving the shooter a very firm hold on the pistol. The

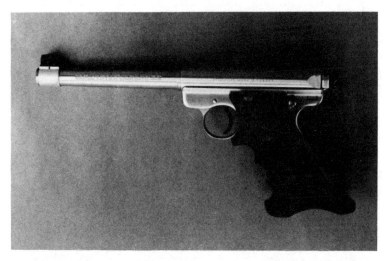

Volquartsen Custom Pistols' excellent "Volthane" fiberglass target grips (shown here on a stainless steel Mark II Target pistol). The Volthane grips have a full target thumb rest, heel rest, and finger grooves.

two side panels are joined by a checkered front strap, which covers the grip frame under the trigger guard. A few shooters with small hands may dislike the extra bulk added to the grip, but most find the Pachmayr grips very comfortable to use. (It should be noted that in "quick draws," which cause a shooter to get a poor hold of his pistol, having a Pachmayr grip assembly can make it hard to adjust to a proper hold since the grips tend to hold onto the skin. This is generally not a problem with those using Ruger pistols, however.) The cost for the Standard/Mark I-style Pachmayr grips is about $27, while the Mark II-style costs a dollar more.

Some shooters may need an inexpensive .22 pistol with a grip angle similar to that of the Browning Hi-Power, Beretta 92, Colt 1911-A1, and a number of other combat automatic pistols. Given the Ruger pistol's availability and low price tag, many will find it ideal for building marksmanship skills with the other, large-bore pistols or in honing instinctive shooting skills. Those hoping to carry out such plans, however, are often disappointed to discover that the Ruger's point of aim is quite different from most 9mm and .45 autos due to its grip angle of about 60 degrees (as opposed to the 70-degree dip found on larger centerfires).

There is a solution to this problem, however. It's the grip designed by Jim Clark, marketed as the Clark 45 adapter grips. The Clark grips have the basic shape and angle of the 1911-A1 so that the point of aim on the Ruger dips down to that of the .45. Those who use any of the new Super Nines with double-row, staggered magazines will find the Clark 45 grips too narrow, but building up the grips with epoxy putty can readily cure this problem. The Clark 45 is available from Brownells for about $20.

Any of the above grips are easy to install. The user simply unscrews the two screws in each grip panel of the pistol, puts the new grips in place, and replaces the screws. Use of gunsmithing screwdrivers is a must for this task if the pistol's screws are to look good.

Sturm, Ruger & Company continues to sell walnut grip panels for about $19.50. These have a thumb groove on the

The Clark 45 grips on this stainless steel Ruger Mark II Bull Barrel have had epoxy putty added to increase their width for use by a Beretta 92 pistol shooter. Also shown is the Red-E Release side lever.

left panel that lefties will dislike. The grips come with the Ruger medallion, which gives them an "official" look on a Ruger pistol. (Interestingly enough, the Ruger falcon medallion, part number XR-52, is sold by the company for about 75 cents. Those wanting to jazz up a non-Ruger grip panel can use a little elbow grease to create a hole in the re-placement grip in order to make the medallion fit.)

Magnum Grips sells walnut target grips for the Mark I and Mark II series of pistols for approximately $20. These are similar to the Sturm, Ruger & Company grips but are available both with and without the thumb rest (lefties, take note).

Finally, those who feel like doing some real do-it-yourself work may wish to experiment with epoxy putty to create their own customized grips. The glue is readily avail-able in most hardware stores and can be molded, as its name suggests, like putty.

To do this type of work, remove the pistol grip panels and magazine, place the four grip screws back onto the frame, and coat the whole grip area with a light covering of wax (so that the putty will readily come free after hardening). When the wax dries, the four grip screws should back out of their holes about halfway.

Next, mix the two halves of the putty together (taking time to read the directions on the package and being aware of any warnings on the container). Place the putty around the pistol grip in roughly the thickness you wish for the final grips; care should be taken that the epoxy gets under the grip screws. That done, grasp the pistol grip tightly for a few seconds with your shooting hand so that the epoxy molds itself around your fingers.

The tricky part comes next: carefully unscrew the screws so they don't stick in the glue. It is wise to clean them in acetone before the glue dries on them. Place the pistol aside for the epoxy to harden (if a lot of putty is used, check it from time to time to be sure it hasn't drooped).

A little file work finishes the new grip; bubble holes or other problems can be filled with the putty. Paint can be used to color the grip. Best results will occur if epoxy paint is used and the paint is added a short time after the putty hardens before it cures completely. Be sure to allow time for the paint to cure. The end result should be a pistol grip which fits the shooter's hand exactly.

MAGAZINES

The original Ruger magazines were a bit hard to insert and reload; they also held only 9 rounds. The new M-10 magazines have been reworked and hold 10 rounds. They are also easier to insert and remove from the gun.

Many complain of the "thumb busting" needed to re-load Ruger magazines, and magazine loaders of various types are seen from time to time. One of the less expensive and more useful of these devices is the Clip-Loader, which costs only about $3.50. This plastic device goes over the top of the magazine and gives the shooter a wide thumb lever to push on rather than the small follower button. It's simple, inexpensive, and works in a straightforward manner.

For those who desire a bit more firepower while hunting (or who might be forced to use a .22 for self-defense), Ram-Line offers a plastic magazine for the Ruger pistols that has a 12-round capacity. The Ram-Line magazine is nearly all plastic; this makes it a lot easier to keep rust-free without using oil. In the Mark IIs, the magazines will hold the slide open after the last round is fired (just like the Ruger magazines). Perhaps the best part of the Ram-Line magazine is that it is easier to load, thanks to a moving, coiled spiral spring rather than the standard wire spring found on the Ruger magazine. Many shooters find the Ram-Line magazines a must for the Ruger pistols; cost per magazine is about $14.50.

Extended magazines for the Ruger pistols aren't currently available. It is possible—though not too practical—to take two standard magazines and remove the base plate of one and the lips of the other, solder them together, grind a magazine-release engagement hole in the back of the combined magazines, and unite the springs of the two to end up with a 16- to 20-round magazine (capacity depending on how well the work is done). This is a lot of work, but it is the only route available until some manufacturer comes out with an extended magazine.

For shooters using the old Standard or Mark I pistols, Brownells offers a magazine Hold-Open follower, which is extra long in order to keep the bolt from closing when the last shot is fired by blocking it open. The follower is made of aluminum so that it won't damage the bolt face, and it reduces the magazine capacity by one round. The followers are sold in pairs with a price tag of about $10 per pair.

MAGAZINE POUCHES

The most delicate part of any automatic pistol is its magazine, and the Ruger pistol is no exception. Fortunately, given a little protection and care, the magazine will give a long life of service.

One way to protect the magazine is to carry spares in a magazine pouch. That way they won't get full of dirt, be accidentally dropped, have their lips bent, or have dings added to their sides.

Uncle Mike's has both single and double magazine pouches which work admirably with the Ruger magazines. The best part is the price: only about $6 each for single pouches and a bit more for the doubles. They come in "designer" black or camouflage. Though designed for Uncle Mike's excellent nylon holster belts, the pouches work fine on most other types of belts as well.

(Uncle Mike's has a number of other pouches and packs which can round out the carrying needs of many backpackers and most hunters. As with Uncle Mike's other products, the tough nylon gear is available in camo and black finishes and is priced very competitively.)

In addition to excellent holsters, belts, and magazine pouches, Uncle Mike's makes a number of tough nylon pouches and "fanny packs" that are of great use for spending a lot of time outdoors. (Photo courtesy of Michaels of Oregon.)

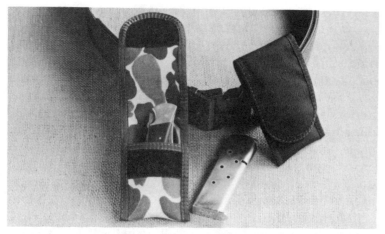

Uncle Mike's magazine pouches can protect as well as carry Ruger magazines. They also make nice pocketknife carriers. (Photo courtesy of Michaels of Oregon.)

MAGAZINE RELEASES

The Ruger pistol's magazine release works well, especially on the new Mark II series. However, if the shooter needs to reload very quickly or is used to reloading a pistol with its release button on the side of the grip rather than the base, he may find the Ruger release not quite to his liking. There are two replacement magazine releases available which deal with these problems in different ways.

The simplest is the nylon Snap Mag Release replacement made by Ram-Line; it extends farther from the base of the grip so that it is more easily pushed. This release makes it possible, with practice, for a shooter to reload as fast as a shooter who has a pistol with a side-mounted release. Care does need to be taken so that the base of the new release doesn't hit anything, since doing so may accidentally release the magazine.

The Ram-Line Snap Mag Release is easy to install. To install, remove the pistol grips, push out the pin holding the release, and mount the new release while the spring powering it is held down. A good gunsmithing screwdriver and needle-nose pliers make the job a snap. The Ram-Line replacement is available for only about $4.

The other aftermarket release is the Thumb Activated Magazine Release from Red-E Products. It gives the shooter a side-mounted release on the left grip in the same position occupied by most other pistols' magazine release buttons.

This unit from Red-E Products has a lever which runs under the inside of the left grip and extends down to a replacement magazine release. Though the action needed to make it function is downward rather than pressing inward on a button (as with most other pistol releases), the two motions are very similar; it seems second nature to shooters used to button magazine releases.

Mounting the replacement release isn't too hard. First, remove the grips and make a small cut in the left grip with a pocketknife or similar tool. Remove the stock magazine release by pushing out its pin, and put the new release into place. Mount the lever on the side of the frame so that it engages the new release, and replace the grips, taking care to place two small washers (that come with the kit) under the bottom-left grip screw.

The only snag you may run into while doing this work is that the spring in the grip of some Rugers is a little short for the release; a quick squeeze with needle-nose pliers to extend the spring's nose will solve this problem. The bottom screw on some grips will seem rather high with the two washers under it; grinding off the screw takes care of this. Finally, the Red-E Products release seems a little long to some who use it; grinding off about a fourth of an inch from its top will cure this problem.

PELLET PISTOLS

There are occasions when the owner of a target version of the Ruger pistol needs to practice but can't, for one reason or another, get to a shooting range or out into the wilds. On such occasions, having a pellet or BB gun that is similar to the Ruger pistol in size and grip angle can be a help in maintaining shooting skills.

There are several pistols available that fit the bill for such shooting. One is the Crosman Mark II, which is a close copy of the Ruger pistols. The gun is powered by a CO_2 cylinder; unlike the old CO_2 pistols which changed their point of impact as the store of gas was depleted from the cylinder, these new ones have more or less constant velocity. The Mark II works with lead pellets or—when shooting on the cheap—BBs, with each pellet or BB being hand-fed or hand-cycled into the chamber. Velocity with pellets is 435 to 485 fps (feet per second), depending on the pellet, making the pistol capable of taking out small pests and being used for target shooting. The cost of the Mark II will vary from store to store, with some discount stores carrying it for less than the suggested retail price of $50.

Daisy's Power Line 1200 is another CO_2 pistol that should also be considered. It has a 60-shot BB magazine and a rear sight that is adjustable for windage and elevation. Muzzle velocity is 420 to 450 fps with BBs gravity-fed for firing. While the grip angle is not quite the same as that of the Ruger pistols, a bit of epoxy putty can be used to "fatten" the area of the grip engaged by the web of the hand in order to make it point like a Ruger. This done, the pistol becomes an excellent practice aid. The Power Line 1200 carries a very competitive price tag of about $32, making it a better buy for many shooters.

For those interested in really honing their shooting skills, Daisy also markets a family of precision air pistols that have single-pump, pneumatic air reservoirs, adjustable rear sights, and rifled steel barrels capable of giving very good accuracy. The only catch is that these, too, have grip angles steeper than that of the Ruger pistol (this angle may come close to that of some target grips that are mounted on some Rugers, however). Again, the old epoxy-putty-in-the-web-of-the-grip ploy can also quickly adapt the pistol grip to the proper angle.

The low end of the price scale of the Daisy family of precision pistols is the Power Line 717. Although the shooter must cock the Power Line 717 (and others in the family) for each shot (unlike the faster fire capabilities of the CO_2 guns when firing BBs), the hassle of buying and replacing gas cylinders all the time is done away with. Muzzle velocity is around 360 fps (depending on the .177-caliber pellet used), and the price tag for the 717 is only about $56.

Two other members of the family have better quality grips and finish and are designed for *very* precise shooting. Daisy's Power Line Match 747 and 777 both have adjustable triggers and Lothan Walther target barrels. The retail price for the 747 is about $110; the 777 lists for around $250.

RWS (Rheinische-Westfälische Sprengstoff, a German ammunition manufacturer) has a number of good spring-powered air pistols one might consider. However, the grip angle on the RWS is rather steep, making the point of aim different from most Rugers except, perhaps, those having very steep target grips. For those who happen to have such grips on a Ruger, the RWS 5G, 6M, or Model 10 (about $125, $220, and $435, respectively) might be worth considering.

REPLACEMENT SIGHTS

The sights on the Mark I and Mark II pistols are excellent and usually best left on the pistol; however, some shooters may wish to tinker with these to change the sight picture. Those wanting to upgrade their Standard pistol models may also benefit by replacing the rear sight.

For Mark I or Mark II pistol owners, one inexpensive way of changing the sight picture is to replace the rear blade of the sight with a white outline rear blade. Such a part is available from Brownells for about $5.45.

Brownells also markets a Ruger elevation screw replacement. Each of these screws has extra "clicks" cut into the rear of its head so that finer adjustments can be made when zeroing the sights; cost is just around $5 for a pack of four.

All of the other replacement sights listed below are also carried by Brownells. Each can be readily installed by simply drifting out the rear sight of the pistol and drifting in the new one. (Occasionally, a bit of file work may be called for to get the sight to fit, but this isn't generally so. Those who may be replacing the original sight back on the pistol should file the new sight to fit the gun rather than the Ruger to fit the new sight, since other sights might be placed on the pistol in the future.)

The MMC Combat Sight is made to fit the Ruger Standard autos. The sight is made both plain and with a white outline around the notch. One good feature is that it is low enough to allow the use of the Standard front sight so that it won't need to be modified or replaced. The MMC sight is adjustable for both windage and elevation by small screws. The cost is about $29 for the base and about $8.55 for a plain sight leaf. The white outlined one sells for around $12.55.

Micro Sights are also available for the Ruger pistols. These are higher than the stock sights on the Ruger; this means that the Micro Sight front blade has to be purchased to replace the Ruger blade; the trade-off is that the sight picture is larger due to the deeper rear notch which can be made with the increased height. The Micro Sights are screw-adjustable in 1/4-minute clicks for both windage and elevation. The cost for the rear sight is about $31.50, while the blade front sight sells for about $8.50.

Millet Adjustable Replacement Sights are offered in models that will fit the Ruger Standard or, with a Millet front sight, the Mark I. With some drilling to create a pinhole, a front sight will fit the Mark II. The rear sight is available in a white-outlined Combat model or in a target version with squared corners. Sights are adjustable for windage and elevation by using a small screwdriver or special Millet sight tool (available from Brownells for about $3.10). Either style of rear sight can be had for about $47.29.

Jim Clark has designed Ruger replacement rear sights for use on the Mark I Bull Barrel T512 and Ruger Mark I 6 7/8-inch barrel T678 models. These wide sight blades have rounded edges to help keep them from getting caught on clothing or in a holster; they are available with a plain sight blade (for about $20) or with a white-outlined blade (about $24).

For those who carry a Bull Barrel Ruger around a lot in a holster, the Sport Site might be of interest. It is available in blued or nickel finish and can easily replace the front sight on the Bull Barrel guns by simply removing the screws, taking off the original front sight, and installing the new sight on the barrel with the original screws. The Sport Site has a conventional rounded front site that, though it doesn't give quite as sharp a sight picture, also doesn't catch or cut into holsters. Cost for the machined steel is about $10; it's available from Engineered Accessories.

Finally, for those who have a Bull Barrel Mark I, it is possible to get a Wichita Rib assembly, which goes over the top of the barrel to create a rib a bit higher than the standard sight picture, with an adjustable rear sight and a small blade at the front. The barrel rib is matte-blued and can be installed without drilling or tapping the barrel. The unit goes for about $90, making it a rather expensive addition with dubious benefits for most shooters.

REPLACEMENT TRIGGERS

It's hard to beat the triggers on the Mark II pistols. Some owners of the old Standard pistols may wish to upgrade the trigger to help obtain better results when target shooting. Many gunsmiths can also smoothen bearing surfaces on the sear, hammer, and disconnector to tune up the pull as well (such work is *not* for anyone but a gunsmith). Machine turning as outlined above might also be of some benefit to steel replacement triggers, though doing so on a Ruger pistol is more for looks than anything else.

Currently, Sturm, Ruger & Company will upgrade a Standard pistol to Mark II specifications for about $26.50 for blued models or about $32 for stainless guns. This work has to be done at Sturm, Ruger & Company's shops, so you'll need to send the pistol via UPS. The work consists of replacing the hammer, sear, and trigger with Mark II parts (with the trigger having the Mark II overtravel stop on it).

Another solution to changing the trigger of a Ruger is

the Jim Clark trigger marketed by Brownells. The trigger is made of stainless steel, and the pinholes in it are carefully reamed so that it doesn't "slop" around. The trigger also has a screw stop to help minimize overtravel. The Clark trigger has a bit lower pull area than do the Ruger triggers, which may also appeal to some shooters; the Clark trigger fits both the Mark I and Mark II series and costs only about $10.

Some shooters may also benefit from having a slack screw placed in the Ruger's trigger guard. This screw is placed at an angle so that its point can push the trigger back and take up any slack before the trigger brings the disconnector up tight against the sear. Coupled with a trigger having overtravel adjustment, this allows minimal trigger movement for very fast repeated firing.

The replacement of the trigger can be done by most Ruger pistol owners, but placement and the threading of a screw hole for a slack screw is best left to a gunsmith.

SCOPE MOUNTS

Most Ruger pistols are accurate enough to merit good scopes. While it is possible to weld or drill, tap, and screw a steel scope base to the top of the receiver, it's a lot of work. For those looking for the lowest possible weight when mounting a scope, this is the best route to take.

The Magnum Pistol Mounts from Brownells are the first choice. They require that three screw holes be drilled and tapped in the Ruger receiver. Once done, the scope is held on the low rib-like mount with Redfield rotary dovetail rings. Styles are available for both Standard, Mark I, and Mark II models and cost about $52.90 each. The mounting work is best done by a gunsmith.

For those who don't mind putting up with a few extra ounces of weight (and a lot less trouble in mounting the scope), it's far easier to simply use the aftermarket pistol scope mounts available; these are relatively inexpensive and can be mounted on the Ruger by the owner with a minimum of fuss.

First choice of the scope mounts are two styles offered by B-Square. One nice feature of both types is that the iron sights can still be used with the scope and mount in place so that, should a scope become damaged, the pistol can still be aimed without taking anything off of it. This could be a very important feature for those using the Ruger pistol as a survival gun or under circumstances where not having the scope work properly would create a major problem.

The B-Square mounts are easy to use. They simply clamp onto the receiver and are held in place by tightening the hex screws with the wrench supplied with them.

B-Square's Mono-Mount is one of the company's top sellers. It has a single wide ring that holds a scope tightly in place. Even though this single ring might not look as strong as a double-ringed arrangement, it's actually quite adequate, especially when using a short pistol scope. It also

B-Square's Mono-Mount, shown here on a Mark I Bull Barrel, has a single wide ring that holds a scope tightly in place. The mount weighs only two ounces. (Photo courtesy of B-Square.)

The dovetail mount from B-Square can be used with standard one-inch rings and a scope or with a dot scope (like the Aimpoint shown here on the Mark II 10-inch Bull Barrel). Sights remain usable with the mount clamped in place. (Photo courtesy of B-Square.)

makes for a lightweight system since the mount only weighs two ounces. Another advantage of these scope mounts is that, with care, the scope can be removed and then remounted later in the same spot on the pistol without losing the scope's zero. This makes removing the scope practical, and replacing it on the pistol is a hassle-free operation. The Mono-Mounts are available in both stainless steel (for around $50) or blued finish (for about $40).

The Dovetail Mount from B-Square uses standard one-inch rings, or it can be used with Aimpoint or similar dot scopes; like B-Square's Mono-Mount, with a little care this one can be taken off and replaced without losing the scope's zero. The unit simply slides over the receiver and is then clamped in place. This mount is also available in stainless (about $60) or blued models (for about $50).

Ciamillo Bases replace the rear sights of the Ruger pistol and then allow standard Weaver-style rings for mounting the scope on the base. These are made of aluminum and are not quite as tough as B-Square's. They are, however, a bit lighter and mount lower for those who don't plan on using iron sights. These are available with either a black or a silver/gray anodized aluminum finish from Brownells for around $43.50 each.

Burris offers a scope mount that replaces the "innards" of the Mark II Ruger adjustable rear sight and uses a ring around the barrel just ahead of the receiver to further steady the mount. The Burris mount can be used with bull barrels or, with the shim insert included with the mount, on tapered barrels. The cost is about $40 for the "silver" mount and around $35 for the blued mounts. The big drawback with these mounts is that they are slow to remove and require disassembling the rear sight to boot. Because of these facts, they should be used only by those who don't plan on ever using iron sights.

About the only negative aspects of using scope mounts and scopes with the Ruger pistol is the weight added to the gun and the surface abrasions that the mounts usually make on the pistols. The added weight isn't too great, however, and a little work with steel wool and (on blued models of the gun) touch-up blue will cure any scratches. For many, the added accuracy potential of the Ruger pistol and the ability to see exactly what is being shot at makes the use of scopes well worth considering. Given the possibility of damaging a scope in the field, scope mounts that leave the iron sights in place have a slight edge over those that replace the sight, except for those shooters incapable of using iron sights or engaged in target shooting requiring a scope.

SCOPES

Modern optical scopes are better and tougher than they were just a few years back, but they are still a bit fragile and must be protected by a good pistol case or large holster when not actually in use.

It's possible to mount a rifle scope on the Ruger and fire it with a cross-armed hold so that the barrel rests in the crook of the off arm. This, however, is not too satisfactory, since it greatly increases the pistol's weight and requires a

bit of time to get off a shot since the position has to be assumed to gain the proper eye relief for the scope picture.
(Too, many find having the rear of the bolt bob toward their
face during recoil quite disconcerting.)

Therefore, most shooters prefer a long-relief optical
scope designed for pistols on their Rugers. While these pistol scopes don't offer very wide fields of view and are generally available only in a few fixed powers, they are light, their
parallax is better suited to pistol use, and the shooter can
hold the pistol in the normal, outreached-arm position.

Most pistol scopes have very low fixed powers, which
are ideal for most pistol shooting (though varminters or
even some hunters may prefer the scopes with higher powers). This is necessary for most handgun shooting since the
field of view is so small that higher powers would make it
hard to quickly find a target. Although it would seem that a
1X, 1.3X, or 1.5X power scope or dot scopes would be little
better than iron sights, they can in fact be a bit quicker at
best. They may be ideal for those who experience some
vision problems.

For very tall shooters with long arms, care must be taken
to get a scope with long enough eye relief. A few pistol
scopes have relatively short eye relief, and shooters with
long arms may discover that the scope doesn't work for
them. Such shooters are well advised to purchase their
scope at a gun store where the scope can be tested rather
than buying it through the mail. Testing is simple; with the
arm outstretched and the hand positioned as if a pistol were
being held, the scope is rested on top of the hand at the V
formed between the base of the thumb and hand. The sight
picture should be full and clear. If it is not, another scope
should be chosen.

Among some of the better readily available pistol scopes
are the Bausch & Lomb 2X and 4X Handgun, Burris 2X and
3X Mikro, Bushnell Phantom (with 1.3X and 2.5X power),
Leupold Extended Eye Relief (2X and 4X power), Redfield
MP (2 1/2X and 4X power), Simmons Handgun (1.3X, 2X,
4X power), Tasco Pistol Scopes (3X and 4X), and the

Thompson/Center Lobo (1.5X, 2.5X, and 3X power). All of these fixed scopes are pretty good. Shooters should *avoid* unknown bargain scopes since they are seldom a bargain; with optical systems, the buyer pretty much gets what he pays for. Quality costs.

Dot scopes that place a dot of light in the field of view in a scope rather than in the cross hairs are also available for use with scope mounts on the Ruger pistols. Even though these scopes aren't a lot faster to use than low-powered optical scopes when shooting with one eye closed, many shooters use dot scopes with both eyes open (which is practical, since the scopes don't magnify the target). This makes it possible to use both eyes to follow a moving target and fire, allowing the shooter a fuller field of view; these can be important considerations when hunting or if in a combat situation. The faster speed the scopes provide in locating a target is the reason most shooters in "combat" contests use a dot scope of one type or another.

One style of dot scope is the occluded eye scope, which creates a dot without any view of the target. To use these scopes, both eyes *must* be open since the shooter's brain combines the picture coming to it from each eye into one sight picture; the dot seen by one eye and the target by the other are superimposed in the mind. With a little practice, using this system is very quick and gives a wide field of view. However, a few people who have vision problems (and some contact-lens wearers) find that the occluded dot scope doesn't work well for them.

The first choice among occluded eye scopes is the Armson OEG (Occluded Eye Gunsight), which costs about $220 for the full-size version with a glow-in-the-dark insert in it. The OEG has a glow-red dot that is small enough not to cover small distant targets but that is easy to find in most backgrounds.

The Armson OEG works with available light, getting brighter as the surrounding light gets brighter; there are no batteries to change, a comfort for some shooters. At night, a small radioactive insert (safely sealed inside the scope) gives it a whitish-green aiming point; while this is a bit hard to see, it works and is certainly better than nothing if a gun must be fired at night.

A number of dot scopes are also available which create electronic dots that are superimposed in the shooter's view through the scope. These scopes are more ideal for those with vision problems in one eye (though they can be used with both eyes open as well). Although the brightness of the electric dot needs to be adjusted manually to match the background brightness in the area it's being used in, these dot scopes give a very good sight picture since both eyes can be open. Finally, on rare occasions when the shooter is firing from a very dark area into a brightly lit one, the electric dot scopes can be turned up to create a brighter dot. The polarizing filter can be turned down to darken the target area. Consequently, once in a great while, the electric dot scopes can find targets that get "washed out" when occluded eye sights are used.

The two best-known brands of electric dot scopes are the Aimpoint (which costs around $180 and seems to be first choice of "combat"-style shooters) and the Tascorama or Battery Dot Sight, from Tasco (it sells for around $180). Many shooters worry that the batteries may fail in one of these scopes at a critical moment; in fact, batteries are readily available and last for up to several thousand hours at the lower scope settings (brighter settings cause the batteries to wear out sooner, and care does need to be taken to turn off the sights when they are stored away). With both brands, the brightness of the light is adjusted with a manually controlled rheostat.

Aimpoint has recently come out with two lightweight electric dot scopes that can be mounted in one-inch scope rings designed for optical scopes. The 2000 Short is especially ideal for use with the B-Square Mono-Mounts. The 2000 Long is designed for use with rifles; though heavier, it will, however, also work on a pistol. Both are available with black or stainless finishes and cost around $180 (though prices vary on these at the time of this writing).

At the time of this writing, Action Arms has introduced a Ruger Mark II mount for its Mark V, Pro V, and Pro 45 scopes (which look suspiciously like the Aimpoint 2000 Short). The scopes also have one-inch bodies so that they will ride in scope mounts designed for optical pistol sights. While the Action Arms scopes don't have any features not found on scopes by Tasco or Aimpoint, some shooters may wish to consider them. The mounts are available by themselves in stainless steel or blued finishes and have a retail price of about $32.

Last and least in price (but not necessarily in quality) is the "bargain basement" dot scope: Daisy's Point Aim scope, which uses available light to reflect a sight picture back at the shooter's eyes as he stares in the direction of his target. It has the advantage of the electric dot scopes in that it can be used with only the master eye or with both eyes open, but it doesn't require batteries since it uses available light. The shooter has a choice of a number of different reticles, including dots, rings, and cross hairs (which are easily removed from the "sticky backed" sheet included with the scope and mounted into place with tweezers).

The Daisy Point Aim scope is made of tough plastic and has .22-size scope mounts molded into its base. This creates a small problem in mounting the scope since most Ruger mounts are for one-inch rings or Weaver bases rather than .22 sized mounts. Also, the Point Aim has problems in dim light when the sight pattern becomes a bit hard to see, which can be a minor consideration for many types of target work. Because the Point Aim is so light, however, the author has seen it mounted successfully to the top of a Ruger pistol with only epoxy cement to hold it in place. Given the Point Aim's price tag of around $15, it makes a very inexpensive and lightweight sighting device worth considering.

A laser can also be used as an aiming device by mounting it on a scope base; this has to be the ultimate high-tech system for a Ruger pistol. Lasers create coherent beams of intense light which travel over long distances without spreading out. Recently, a number of lasers have been marketed that are small and tough enough to be mounted on a rifle and used as aiming devices.

Using a laser system is simple: the laser beam is "zeroed" so its beam hits at the same point as a bullet strikes (for the Ruger, at 25 or 50 yards). The pistol can then be fired from the hip (or wherever) by just holding it steady and, when the dot of light created by the laser is on target, squeezing off a shot. The bullet strikes within inches of where the dot of light hits over the useful range of the .22 LR; compensating for the bullet drop at longer ranges makes 100-yard-plus shots practical without bringing the pistol up to sight it in the normal manner.

Unfortunately, lasers aren't without their shortcomings. The major drawback is that a laser dot is virtually invisible in bright sunlight. This limits its use to indoors, or outdoors during twilight or the night. (Lasers can be seen by night-vision equipment or even a person downrange, making such an aiming system less than ideal for some types of combat applications. The .22 LR is, of course, already less than ideal for most combat.)

There have recently been a number of companies which have introduced small lasers having reasonable price tags of only $250 to $500. Among the best is the Lasersight LS 45, which is manufactured in England and distributed in the United States by Avin Industries. These little units are easily mounted on the B-Square Dovetail Mount listed above.

SILENCERS

Silencers have gotten a bad rap in the United States. Although readily available in many European countries (often despite very stiff gun laws), the majority of the public in the States has been successfully brainwashed by Hollywood and others into seeing these devices as being of use to only criminals. Consequently, silencers have been banned in a number of states, while the federal government heavily regulates and taxes those which are legally owned elsewhere in the United States. Meanwhile, in Europe and other countries, silencers are used by sportsmen in low-crime populations who value the idea of not making a lot of racket when hunting or target shooting.

At any rate, the standard .22 LR cartridge is ideally suited for use in a firearm with a sound suppressor since most fire .22 bullets which move at subsonic speeds, creating only a small muzzle blast even when unsilenced. (This is not the case with supersonic bullets like those shot from the new "high-velocity" or "hyper-velocity" rounds, which create a supersonic crack when traveling through the air.)

Silencers can, of course, be used for illegal purposes, and they are. But then so are some firearms and a lot of other devices. There is reason to believe that a number of silenced weapons have been used in combat and clandestine activities from time to time. By virtue of its accuracy, reliability, and stationary, exposed barrel, the Ruger pistol is ideal for such use and has therefore often been coupled with a silencer in such operations.

Although the High Standard was apparently used by the OSS during World War II and the CIA following the war, various elements in the U.S. Government and the military discovered that Ruger pistols were more dependable than the High Standard or similar .22s. Therefore, the Ruger, equipped with a silencer, was occasionally used in the Vietnam War to root out the Vietcong in tunnels.

Perhaps the best known of the modified pistols used in Vietnam is the Ruger/MAC Mk1 pistol, which was a standard Mark I pistol modified by Mitchell WerBell III and Gordon Ingram at WerBell's MAC (Military Armament Corporation)—a company that also turned out a number of other innovative weapons, such as the MAC-10 submachine guns. The suppressed Ruger had an integral silencer over its thin barrel and was constructed so that it looked nearly identical to the standard Ruger Bull Barrel model. The silencer itself measured 5.5 inches and used a baffle design of stainless steel discs. The total weight of the pistol was 2.56 pounds, with the overall dimensions being the same as those of the standard Bull Barrel version of the Mark I.

Although it is unknown exactly when and where the

Ruger/MAC Mk1 was used following its introduction in the mid 1960s, it was tested at Aberdeen Proving Ground, Eglin Air Force Base, Coronado (by the Navy SEALs), Ft. Benning, Ft. Bragg, and Rock Island Arsenal, which suggests that the U.S. Army, Navy, Air Force, and, undoubtedly, the CIA all used the pistol to some extent.

Since the Vietnam War, a number of companies took the lead from MAC so that silenced Ruger pistols are now readily available legally to those who can legally own such pistols.

(It should be noted that many people mistake bull-barreled Rugers for silenced weapons—a fact that bemused owners of the pistols often don't bother to correct. Consequently, it would seem probable that some of the "silenced" Rugers which one sometimes hears about are only bull-barreled guns.)

Currently, Jonathan Arthur Ciener is probably the best-known person making silencers for the Mark Is and IIs. The Ciener silencers are integral (i.e., built around the pistol's barrel), giving very good results and doing away with problems in getting the silencer aligned with the barrel. The cost for one of Jonathan Arthur Ciener's reworked Mark II pistols with a silencer is about $412 for a blued model and about $457 for a stainless steel model. The Mark II KMK-10 version is available for around $600. Government taxes on the weapons will run up additional costs.

Readers needing a silencer should get a legally manufactured unit such as Jonathan Arthur Ciener's, since such commercial units work well; do-it-yourself silencers and kits, usually don't work nearly as well and are difficult to make.

For those wanting to confound their buddies or pretend to own a silencer, there is the Fake Silencer made by Daniel Manufacturing which mounts on the Cobray threaded barrels used to mount real silencers on Ruger pistols. The fake suppressor costs around $20; the barrel goes for about $48 from Specialized Weapons Distributors (see Appendix A).

As mentioned above, replacing the barrel of a Ruger destroys the original barrel and is a job for a gunsmith; given the trouble and expense, most Ruger owners would be better advised to purchase a bull-barreled model of the Ruger and tape some contact paper on its barrel or glue an aluminum shroud to it if they need to pretend they have a silencer. (Note: The .22 CB Cap Long makes only a slight report when fired from a 10-inch bull barrel, thereby giving "realism" to a make-believe silencer for those into such games.)

STORAGE CASES

Carrying cases, or pistol rugs as they're commonly called in the business, protect a pistol from getting scuffed and nicked if it is stored in a closet or car trunk for long periods. It's important that air circulate through such a storage bag so that moisture doesn't condense inside the case and rust or tarnish the gun; vinyl cases are especially prone to this problem and are best avoided.

A case is also ideal when a shooter is carrying a pistol to and from a car or through a populated area, since it is less apt to alarm people than a visible pistol. Hard plastic and aluminum cases are a must if a shooter is transporting a pistol on commercial airplanes. Anyone doing so should be sure to check regulations well before the trip and should insist that clerks not put an identifying tag on the outside of the case if at all possible).

The best source of gun rugs and cases is a local gun store, since it is possible to inspect the case for quality and check its size before purchase.

Chapter 5

Ammunition

The .22 LR rimfire cartridge is the most popular one in the world. No matter where a person travels, providing ammunition ownership isn't banned, it's possible to purchase .22 LR rounds. Some smaller .22 rounds can be hand-cycled through the Ruger pistol, and a few target pistols are chambered for the .22 Short. All in all, there is a wealth of ammunition to choose from when it comes to stoking Ruger pistols.

Care should be taken when choosing ammunition, however. Good ammunition, with bullets capable of handling the job they are called upon to do, can make a big difference in a .22's effectiveness. Good ammunition will cause less fouling of the Ruger pistol and will function more reliably. Quality ammunition can also quickly bring down a small-game animal or will create smaller groups on the range. Bad ammunition, or the wrong type for the job at hand, will give poor results.

Currently, U.S. companies like Olin/Winchester, Federal Cartridge Company, Omark/CCI, and Remington are *the* companies offering quality ammunition at reasonable prices. They also offer inexpensive plinking ammunition which isn't corrosive though it often causes a lot of fouling because of the lubricant on the bullets.

Shooters should avoid corrosive, imported ammunition at all costs. Although there isn't much of this on the market these days, it's still occasionally encountered. If in doubt, throw it out. A corrosive round used in a Ruger pistol can really trash the bore if it isn't cleaned shortly after firing.

Two companies currently importing quality noncorrosive .22 ammunition are Hansen Cartridge Company (generally importing from European manufacturers) and PMC (from South Korea). These companies often offer a lot of quality with slightly lower price tags than are found with American-made ammunition making the cartridges especially ideal for those looking for inexpensive plinking or practice rounds.

Bearing in mind the fact that an entire book would be needed to cover the ammunition available for firing in a Ruger pistol, here's a small sampling of the wide variety of .22 ammunition currently available to most shooters in the United States.

.22 SHORT

As mentioned earlier, a number of Rugers have been re-barreled for the .22 Short, which is used in some target shooting. The round can be used in .22 LR pistols as well, but this is not really satisfactory since it will not function in a semiauto action, though it will chamber. With extensive or prolonged use, it might even cause chamber erosion. For these reasons, along with the fact that it is also usually more expensive to purchase the .22 Short than the .22 LR, using the Short makes it less than ideal for such use except in a real pinch.

Some shooters use the .22 Short in .22 LR pistols because the report produced is softer than that of the larger shell. A much better choice for quiet shooting is the .22 CB Long Cap (see below) since it is even softer. Because of its extra length, it won't produce barrel erosion.

Among the more accurate .22 Short rounds are CCI's Short Target, Remington's Target, and RWS' R-25 Match (imported into the United States by Dynamite Nobel).

For those wishing to use the .22 Short for hunting with a Ruger chambered for .22 Short, CCI's Mini-Mag gives a bit more energy in this chambering and is available in a hollow-point bullet.

.22 MINI CB CAP

This round has the overall length of the .22 Short while having the ballistics of the .22 CB Long (see below). As such, it might be of use to those having a Ruger target pistol chambered for the .22 Short. Otherwise, it would make more sense to use the standard .22 CB Long.

.22 LONG

The .22 Long is an outdated cartridge that now bridges the gap in power between the .22 Short and .22 LR. Like the .22 Short, the .22 Long will chamber in the Ruger pistol, but it lacks the accuracy of the .22 LR, won't consistently cycle the action (unless the recoil spring is cut down or replaced by a weaker spring), and generally costs as much or more than the .22 LR. All these considerations make it a very inferior choice to the .22 LR.

.22 CB LONG CAP

The .22 CB Cap (or similar rounds) was often used in shooting galleries in the early 1900s. The round's soft report and low velocity made it ideal for indoor shooting or when shooting in areas where the noise created by standard rounds would be annoying.

Over the years, the need for the .22 CB Cap decreased until the round was finally discontinued in the mid 1900s, except for a few European countries, which still made short runs of the cartridge. In the United States, it was nearly impossible to find the round, and its importation from Europe created a high enough price tag to keep even the few who wanted the round from purchasing it.

All this changed in the early 1970s. At that time, CCI revived the idea with the introduction of its .22 CB Long Cap. This cartridge was changed in its size; it now has a brass case that is identical to that of the Long Rifle. The longer case makes it possible to use it in guns chambered for the .22 LR cartridge without chambering problems or any problem with chamber erosion with extended use.

As sanctioned shooting areas become harder to find, demand has grown for the low-powered .22 CB Long Cap. In 1988, Federal Cartridge Company and Remington followed CCI's lead and created their own versions (the .22 Long CB Cap for Federal and the CBee22 for Remington). Each is nearly identical with lubricated lead bullets of 29 or 30 grains, low muzzle velocity, and minimal report from a long pistol barrel (and nearly no report from a rifle barrel).

The big plus of the .22 CB Long Cap is that it can be used in a Ruger pistol with only minimal ear protection—even indoors in areas that are properly ventilated. With the MK-10 Bull Barrel version of the Ruger, shooting is quiet enough outdoors to not even require any ear protection.

The .22 CB Long Cap doesn't cycle the action of a .22 LR pistol. This makes it ideal for training beginners, since an accidental second shot can't be fired without hand-cycling the action of the gun. The low report and nearly complete lack of recoil are also important pluses in training beginners.

.22 SHOTSHELL

CCI currently offers a .22 LR Mini-Mag Shotshell, which might be of some use to Ruger pistol shooters.

The CCI shell has a plastic capsule of #12 shot, which occupies the position normally taken by a bullet in .22 ammunition. The rounded capsule eliminates chambering problems. Upon firing, the pistol's rifling tears into the plastic capsule so that it breaks away and is blown clear of the muzzle, releasing the small swarm of shot pellets that travel on toward the target while air resistance makes the capsule quickly drop away just ahead of the muzzle.

This system works well. The catch comes in the small amount of shot that can be used in a .22 LR-size cartridge and in the fact that the rifling imparts centrifugal force, which causes the shot to spread out quickly. (Even though the solution to the latter problem would be a smooth-bore barrel, for rather nebulous reasons, such pistols are illegal to own without a special permit in the United States.)

The shot spread, coupled with the low amount of energy each pellet has (and quickly loses), makes these shot shells less than ideal for self-defense. The round, however, might be of use to those needing a close-range shot pattern to deal with hard-to-hit targets (such as small pests or snakes). One plus of using these rounds in a pistol is that patterns are actually an inch or two smaller than when used with a rifle (though the energy is a bit less for each pellet). This creates a greater number of hits on any given target, so that a disabling hit is more apt to occur on a pest that is shot at close range.

Pattern size will be around five inches at seven feet and will spread to sixteen inches at twenty feet. Given the small number of pellets in the shot load, using the rounds much beyond seven feet becomes a doubtful proposition on a per-shot basis.

One area where the shot cartridges do shine is in shooting aerial targets. Since firing a standard .22 bullet into the air is a very risky proposition because the bullet comes back down with enough force to injure someone, shot shells are the answer for those who wish to knock thrown targets out of the air. Such endeavors can also be useful in gaining quick shooting skills, though the principle reason for engaging in aerial shooting is simply for the fun of it.

.22 LONG RIFLE

The .22 LR was developed in 1887 and was originally loaded with black powder. While the .22 LR and most of the .22 rimfire family made a successful transition from black powder to smokeless powder during the early 1900s, dozens of larger rimfired cartridges didn't do so and were replaced with easily reloaded centerfire rounds. Currently, *billions* of .22 LR rounds are cranked out each year worldwide, making it the most popular round ever invented.

Although the case of the standard .22 LR round is the same length as that of the .22 Long, its bullet is larger, thereby making the overall length of the .22 LR greater.

Two different bullet configurations (hollow-point and solid), as well as several power/velocity groupings, give the shooter a large number of choices when it comes to selecting .22 LR cartridges. Because the Ruger pistol functions well with a wide range of ammunition, the great variety of .22 LR cartridges also allows a shooter to select ammunition that will suit a number of different purposes. In effect, this can make the Ruger pistol a multiuse gun simply by changing the ammunition. A pistol can be a superaccurate target pistol, a small-game hunting pistol, an inexpensive plinker, or even a make-do defensive arm.

It should be noted that the .22 LR's abilities as a defensive round are often exaggerated, both pro and con. In fact, it is capable of being used as a defensive round and has often been so used successfully. In many loadings, the modern .22 LR is actually more effective than the .25 ACP and most .32 ACP rounds. And the round has been effectively used by hit men and, in all probability, in covert action by the United States military and CIA. It has also seen use in other countries.

At the same time, the .22 LR certainly isn't the be-all and end-all for self-defense. This is because it doesn't quickly take an opponent out of action unless the bullet chances to hit the spinal column, brain, or another major organ. Though the round kills more people in the United States than any other, it should be remembered that huge numbers of these cartridges are in use, and those killed don't necessarily die quickly.

Those using the .22 LR in a Ruger or any other firearm

in combat must depend on either an element of surprise (so that the opponent doesn't have time to retaliate and a carefully placed shot can be made), firing shots at very close range so that they can be carefully placed (always a doubtful proposition in real combat), or—more often—sheer, blind luck. In short, most shooters in a combat situation will choose a more potent round if possible.

For maximum damage to a living target, while hunting or in combat, rounds with maximum velocity and expanding HP (hollow-point) bullets are called for. These rounds are generally marketed as "hyper-velocity" cartridges because their bullets travel faster than other .22s. Among the best of these are Federal's HP Spitfires, Winchester's Super-Max, the PMC Hyper Vel, and CCI's Stinger, with the Stinger having a slight edge over the others. These hyper-velocity rounds are the first choice for hunting game at the large end of the "small game" scale or for make-do defensive rounds.

All of these rounds have a slightly longer-than-normal case, which allows more powder to be packed into it; a lighter-than-normal (usually around 32-grain) HP jacketed bullet is then used to top the round. The combination of greater powder and lighter bullet results in a higher muzzle velocity, giving the bullet more power and greater bullet expansion. The bullet then expends its energy within most small game rather than penetrating through it (as does a solid bullet). On the flip side, these rounds do so much damage that it is difficult to harvest meat from smaller game since the bullet actually destroys a lot of the meat; for small game, a solid-point .22 bullet is best.

One might imagine that hyper-velocity cartridges would all be superior to the old-style, heavy lead .22 bullets at longer ranges, but this isn't the case. Because the light hyper-velocity bullets lose their speed faster than do heavier bullets, they start to lose power faster than heavier bullets at around 80 to 100 yards; heavier bullets maintain a greater speed beyond this range, translating into more power.

Of course, it must be remembered that .22 bullets, whether hyper-velocity or standard, are all quite marginal at ranges beyond 80 yards, especially with the short barrels of most Ruger pistols. Because of this, shooters won't be very successful at using their pistols at such extended ranges regardless of the type of bullet being fired. (While the .22 LR is capable of hitting targets out to 200 yards in the hands of a skilled shooter, the bullet doesn't have enough energy to do much damage at such ranges. Shooters who've targeted tin cans at 200 yards will discover that the bullet only dents the thin metal and will not penetrate it. A shooter might score a lucky "knockout punch" on game at 200 yards, but it would not be a very likely bet; the potential for merely wounding the game would make it an undesirable proposition at best.)

The next step down in power from hyper-velocity rounds is the high-velocity .22 LR ammunition. This must not be confused with high-velocity centerfire rifle ammunition; the .22 bullet is high-velocity only if compared to the older standard style of .22 ammunition and doesn't approach the 2,000 fps normally associated with high-velocity bullets.

The high-velocity type of .22 LR ammunition generally has an HP bullet with a metallic jacket to reduce barrel fouling. This cartridge is ideal for many types of hunting (where it creates less damage to meat than the hyper-velocity round). The HP bullet is also less apt to ricochet than the standard FMJ or lead bullets, an important consideration in some areas.

The most common type of .22 LR ammunition is the "standard" cartridge, which has a round-nosed, lubricated lead bullet. Most of this ammunition is inexpensive to purchase, making it ideal for practice, and will work for some types of hunting. Several companies offer small kits that allow the lead bullets to be "hollow-pointed" by using a small drill to place a hole in the nose of the bullet. Such modification of lead bullets is a lot of work if very many are to be altered, and the expansion created by such modification can be disappointing.

Because these rounds are cranked out in great numbers, with an eye to keeping their prices down, bullets of this ammunition are occasionally a bit loose, and powder charges and bullet weights can vary a bit from round to round. The powder and lubricants used in the rounds are also apt to foul a pistol with extended use. All these points make these rounds less than ideal for use where reliable functioning of the firearm over extended time is needed and when it might be impossible to clean the Ruger (i.e., in a survival situation or for self-defense). These cartridges are great for inexpensive practice, however.

Several types of target or "match" .22 LR are available as well. These are rather expensive when compared to other .22 LR rounds, but the results can be very good in Ruger target pistol models. Shooters needing extra accuracy have a wide variety of ammunition to choose from. Among the most accurate rounds to try are Winchester's R1 Match; Federal's Champion Target; Remington's Target; CCI's Competition Green Tag, Mini Group, and Pistol Match; PMC's Match Rifle and Standard Vel. Target; and RWS' Target and Pistol Match cartridges. Also good are Eley Match and Club cartridges, when they can be found.

Several tricks can be used to shrink group sizes with standard ammunition. One is to experiment with different brands of ammunition to see whether a pistol prefers a certain type. Many Ruger pistols will fire tighter groups with some brands of standard ammunition than with others, and the best brand can vary from gun to gun.

While bargain-brand ammunition of unknown origin will almost always give inferior results, purchasing several boxes of each type of the less-expensive CCI, Federal, and/ or Winchester offerings and then trying each for accuracy and functioning in any given pistol may give surprisingly small groups with some pistols. (Generally, standard-velocity ammunition, which sends its bullet out at subsonic speeds, gives best accuracy when fired from a .22 pistol.)

Another hint in gaining maximum accuracy from standard ammunition is to immediately return back to the store where ammunition was purchased if it proves to be very accurate in any given gun. Once there, the shooter should buy up as much of the same case lot as he will need in the near future. Ammunition can vary ever so slightly from one lot to the next as can pistols; purchasing all of one run may help to guarantee that bullets will all strike consistently at the same point of aim.

One interesting trick used by some target shooters is to weigh .22 ammunition and remove any rounds that are heavier or lighter than their companions. The thinking here is that brass is the most consistently made component in ammunition; cartridges weighing more or less than others in a lot probably do so because the bullet is a slightly different size or the powder charge isn't right. Removing these oddballs can noticeably shrink the size of groups fired by a Ruger pistol.

Many standard-velocity rounds are also useful in silencer-equipped Ruger pistols because the bullet is subsonic making it quieter to fire. Hyper-velocity and high-velocity .22 ammunition, even when fired from a silenced Ruger, will be noisy, since the bullets often travel above the speed of sound and make a sonic crack as they cut through the air.

.22 SHORT MAGNUM

If history continues to repeat itself, it would seem to be only a matter of time before someone creates a .22 LR round with even more power than the hyper-velocity rounds. One place such work is currently taking place is at ILARCO (Illinois Arms Company), which is trying to create a more powerful round for use in its AM-180 rifle. It would also seem probable that other major ammunition-manufacturing companies are also engaged in such projects.

Although there is no industrial standardized name for the round yet, ILARCO is calling its round the .22 Short Magnum. If the company is first to market the round, that will probably be the name that will stick. The experimental cartridge has the same overall length as the .22 LR cartridge. When fully developed, it is hoped to have the power of the .22 WMR.

The Ruger pistols are quite tough, and it would seem probable that they might be adapted to use with this cartridge by simply placing a more powerful recoil spring in them (though a heavier bolt also might be called for, depending on the characteristics of the final .22 Short Magnum cartridge).

The beauty of a magnum cartridge with overall dimensions of a standard .22 LR cartridge is that magazines and barrels would all work with the round without needing any modification. The down side is that such a round might cause damage to some older rifles or pistols in which it was accidentally substituted for a standard .22 LR cartridge and fired. Of such stupidity lawsuits are made, and this might be enough to discourage the introduction of such a round.

Another shortcoming would be that the shorter pistol barrels might not be capable of realizing much advantage in velocity over standard .22 LR ammunition. If this were the case, substituting the new, more powerful magnum round for the common, less-expensive .22 LR might not realize enough advantage to make it worth the effort.

If more power could be realized by such a round in a pistol and *if* the Ruger could be readily adapted to the round's use, such a combination would extend the useful range of the Ruger pistol somewhat and also increase the size of game it could harvest. It could also improve the Ruger pistol's self-defense capability.

Only time will tell as to whether or not this round, and any subsequent modifications needed to the Ruger pistol so that such rounds can be used, will prove to be practical.

****

The following table gives the more common specifications for various types of .22 ammunition that may be fired from some versions of the Ruger pistols. It should be noted that these specifications can vary greatly from manufacturer to manufacturer, from country to country, and according to the length of the barrel on the Ruger being used. All the figures shown are approximate and near the maximum; for exact figures, the user should check literature supplied by the manufacturer of the specific brand of ammunition in question, taking careful note of the barrel length used in test-firing.

Specifications for .22 Rimfired Cartridges

Name	Bullet Weight (grains)	Overall Length (in.)	Muzzle Velocity (FPS)	Muzzle Energy (FPE)
.22 Short	29	0.676	1,132	83
.22 Long	29	0.880	1,180	90
.22 CB Long Cap	29	0.883	727	33
.22 Shot Shell	—	0.981	950	—
.22 LR (Standard)	40	0.981	1,138	116
.22 LR (High-Vel.)	40	0.981	1,255	140
.22 LR (Hyper-Vel.)	32	0.981	1,640	191
.22 Magnum Short	40	0.981	*	*

* Experimental round; exact figures unknown at time of this writing.

Manufacturers

Action Arms, Ltd.
P.O. Box 9573
Philadelphia, PA 19124
(Importer of Mark V, Pro 45, and Pro V electric dot scopes
   and mounts for Mark II pistols)

Aimpoint USA
203 Elden St., Suite 302
Herndon, VA 22070
(Aimpoint electric dot scopes)

AMT (Arcadia Machine & Tool)
536 N. Vincent Ave.
Covina, CA 91722
(Manufacturer of "Lightning" pistol)

Armson
P.O. Box 2130
Farmington Hills, MI 48018
(Armson OEG available-light dot scope)

Assault Accessories
P.O. Box 8994
Tucson, AZ 85738
(Manufacturer of the "Assistant" shoulder stock)

Avin Industries
1847 Camino Palmero
Hollywood, CA 90046
(Distributor of "LS45" laser-sighting system)

L.L. Baston Company
P.O. Box 1995
El Dorado, AR 71730
(Distributor of Mini-Lite mount, cleaning kits, and military
    surplus-type gear)

Brigade Quartermasters
1025 Cobb International Blvd.
Kennesaw, GA 30144
(Military surplus-style equipment and accessories and
    Gargoyle glasses)

Brownells, Inc.
Route 2, Box 1
Montezuma, IA 50171
(Distributor of Ruger pistol replacement sights, scope
    mounts, etc., and gunsmithing tools)

B-Square Company
P.O. Box 11281
Fort Worth, TX 76109
(Scope mounts for Ruger pistols)

Bushnell Optical Co.
2828 E. Foothill Blvd.
Pasadena, CA 91107
(Pistol scope)

Choate Machine & Tool
Box 218
Bald Knob, AR 72010
(Manufacturer of firearms accessories)

Clip-Loader, Inc.
5906 S.E. Lloyd St.
Milwaukie, OR 97222
(Manufacturer of "Clip-Loader" Ruger magazine reloader)

Daisy Manufacturing Company
P.O. Box 220
Rogers, AR 72757
(Makers of air guns suitable for practice)

Douglas Barrels, Inc.
5504 Big Tyler Rd.
Charleston, WV 25313
(Barrel blanks for Ruger pistols)

Dynamite Nobel of America, Inc.
105 Stonehurst Court
Northvale, NJ 07647
(Importer of RWS ammunition)

Federal Cartridge Corp.
2700 Foshay Tower
Minneapolis, MN 55402
(Manufacturer of .22 ammunition)

J&G Sales, Inc.
440 Miller Valley Rd.
Prescott, AZ 86301
(Distributor of "Steady Grip")

Jonathan Arthur Ciener, Inc.
6850 Riverside Dr.
Titusville, FL 32780
(Manufacturer of silencers)

Jones Optical
6367 Arapahoe Rd.
Boulder, CO 80303
(Polycarbonate glasses and combat goggles)

La Paloma Marketing
1735 E. Ft. Lowell Rd., Suite #7
Tucson, AZ 85719
(Distributor of "Red-E" magazine release)

Magnum Grips
Box 801
Payson, AZ 85547
(Maker of walnut target grips for Mark I and Mark II)

Michaels of Oregon ("Uncle Mike's")
P.O. Box 13010
Portland, OR 97213
(Manufacturer of nylon holsters)

Olin
Winchester Group
120 Long Ridge Rd.
Stamford, CT 06904
(Manufacturer of Winchester .22 ammunition)

Omark Industries
P.O. Box 856
Lewiston, ID 83501
(Manufacturer of CCI .22 ammunition)

Ram-Line, Inc.
15611 West 6th Ave.
Golden, CO 80401
(Manufacturer of plastic magazines and Snap Mag Release
    for Ruger pistols)

Rheinische-Westfälische Sprengstoff (RWS)
(German ammunition manufacturer)

Ruger Collectors Association, Inc.
P.O. Box 290
Southport, CT 06490

Sherwood International
18714 Parthenia St.
Northridge, CA 91324
(Source for cleaning equipment and military surplus gear)

Sierra Supply
P.O. Box 1390
Durango, CO 81301
(Source for cleaning equipment and Break-Free CLP)

Specialized Weapons Distributors, Inc.
P.O. Box 546
Smyrna, GA 30081
(Distributor of "Fake" silencer and Cobray silencer
    replacement barrel for Ruger pistols)

Sturm, Ruger and Company
Southport, CT 06490
(Manufacturers of Ruger pistols)

Tasco Sales, Inc.
P.O. Box 520080
Miami, FL 33152
(Pistol scope and electric dot scope)

Volquartsen Custom Pistols
P.O. Box 271
Carroll, IA 51401
(Manufacturer of custom grips; custom gunsmithing work
    on Ruger pistols)

Publications and Videotapes

The following books and magazines have valuable information of interest to those needing more information about new products and developments in regard to the Ruger Mark I and II or other Ruger firearms, ammunition, and other related subjects.

American Rifleman magazine
1600 Rhode Island Ave., NW
Washington, DC 20036

Automatics: Fast Firepower,
Tactical Superiority
By Duncan Long
Paladin Press
P.O. Box 1307
Boulder, CO 80306

Conversations with Bill Ruger
(Video Cassette Tape)
Blacksmith Corp.
Box 424
Southport, CT 06490

Deadly Weapons
(Video Cassette Tape)
Anite Productions
P.O. Box 375
Pinole, CA 94564

Firepower magazine
Turbo Publishing
P.O. Box 518
Cottonwood, AZ 86326

Gun Digest
(current issue—yearly publication)
Edited by Ken Warner
DBI Books
4092 Commercial Ave.
Northbrook, IL 60062

The Mini-14: The Plinker, Hunter, Assault,
and Everything Else Rifle
By Duncan Long
Paladin Press
P.O. Box 1307
Boulder, CO 80306

Silencers for Hand Firearms
By Siegfried F. Huebner
Paladin Press
P.O. Box 1307
Boulder, CO 80306

Silencers in the 1980s:
Great Designs, Great Designers
By J. David Truby
Paladin Press
P.O. Box 1307
Boulder, CO 80306

Silencers, Snipers and Assassins
By J. David Truby
Paladin Press
P.O. Box 1307
Boulder, CO 80306

If you liked this book, you will also want to read these:

HANDBOOK OF HANDGUNS
A Comprehensive Evaluation of Military, Police, Sporting, and Personal-Defense Pistols
by Timothy J. Mullin

Not since Elmer Keith's classic *Sixguns* has one book offered so much information on handguns! Here Mullin takes pistols into the 21st century with provocative chapters on modifications, "desperation" weapons, the surplus scene, essential reading, traveling abroad with a handgun, shooting schools and more. 8 1/2 x 11, softcover, photos, 240 pp.   **#10013985**

THE RIGHT TO KEEP AND BEAR ARMS
U.S. Senate Report

This little-known U.S. Senate report is potent ammo for all gun owners interested in the preservation of our right to keep and bear arms. It is proof that the U.S. government itself has studied the meaning of the Second Amendment from all perspectives and concluded that every private citizen has the *individual* right to own and carry firearms in a peaceful manner. 8 1/2 x 11, softcover, 160 pp.   **#10014090**

THE TRUTH ABOUT HANDGUNS
Exploding the Myths, Hype, and Misinformation
by Duane Thomas

Every gun enthusiast will enjoy reading this lively look at the myths about the Colt .45; the hype surrounding handgun stopping power; the truth about Alvin York's incredible World War I firefight; the answers to the questions "Are revolvers dead?" and "How good is the .40 Smith & Wesson cartridge?"; and much more. 5 1/2 x 8 1/2, softcover, 136 pp.   **#10008894**

HAND CANNONS
The World's Most Powerful Handguns
by Duncan Long

"Hand cannons" are the biggest, loudest, most powerful handguns in the shooting world, firing cartridges from the famous .44 Magnum up to the mammoth .50 BMG. Duncan Long evaluates these massive pistols and reveals how to tame their recoil and muzzle blast and improve their accuracy. 5 1/2 x 8 1/2, softcover, photos, illus., 208 pp.   **#10001568**

GLOCK
The New Wave in Combat Handguns
by Peter Alan Kasler

This book debunks the myths, lays to rest the rumors and, through photos of a special cutaway Glock that clearly display its unique inner mechanisms, demystifies the design and operations of what is surely the most innovative handgun introduced in some time – and possibly in the history of handguns. 5 1/2 x 8 1/2, hardcover, photos, illus., 304 pp.   **#10004570**